QUOTES ARE TREMENDOUS!

ISBN: 0-937539-12-0

Goethe ------ Emerson ------ Seneca ------ Disraeli
Shakespeare ----- Tozer ----- Spurgeon

QUOTES

ARE

TREMENDOUS

Edited by

Charles "T" Jones

Executive Books
Publishers

Patton ----- Lincoln ----- Churchill ----- Wanamaker ----- Carnegie
Sheen ---- Chambers ----- Moody

Dedicated

To

Og Mandino

He quotes often
and is
often quoted

INTRODUCTION

Quotes Are Tremendous

Whether you are a general inspiring your troops, a teacher educating a student, a father or mother lecturing your child, a salesperson making a point, a preacher moving your congregation or a speaker motivating an audience, there is nothing that can empower you more than a Tremendous quote.

If you want to get their attention quickly and be remembered, begin with a Tremendous quote, end with a Tremendous quote and season your remarks with Tremendous quotes.

I began reading quotes thirty-five years ago and now my name is mentioned around the world because of my repeating a quote I read in a book written over one hundred years ago and heard repeated by Mac McMillen forty years ago:

"You are the same today as you'll be five years from now except for two things, the people you meet and the books you read."

A Tremendous quote never gets stale and it becomes more a part of you every time you quote it.

Read and reread a few autobiographies. This will give you a greater appreciation for the quote because you know the life it came from. Two of my favorites are Lincoln and Chambers. Everything I say is flavored by their wisdom.

Begin now to memorize a few Tremendous quotes. Repeat them to yourself aloud at every opportunity. Repeat them with feeling and enthusiasm. This will make a Tremendous difference in you, and your listeners will reward you with attentive minds, hungry hearts and warm smiles.

TREMENDOUS

QUOTES

TO

EXCITE, CHALLENGE,

EDUCATE, ENCOURAGE,

COMFORT & HUMBLE

EDITED BY

CHARLES 'T' JONES

TREMENDOUS QUOTES ON QUOTES

I have somewhere seen it observed that we should make the same use of a book that the bee does of a flower; she steals sweets from it, but does not injure it.--Colton

The art of quotation requires more delicacy in the practice than those conceive who can see nothing more in a quotation than an extract. --Disraeli

The adventitious beauty of poetry may be felt in the greater delight with a verse given in happy quotation than in the poem.--Emerson

A great man quotes bravely, and will not draw on his invention when his memory serves him with a word as good.--What he quotes he fills with his own voice and humor, and the whole cyclopedia of his table-talk is presently believed to be his own.--Emerson

I pluck up the goodlisome herbs of sentences by pruning, eat them by reading, digest them by musing, and lay them up at length in the high seat of memory by gathering them together; that so, having tasted their sweetness, I may the less perceive the bitterness of life. --Queen Elizabeth

One must be a wise reader to quote wisely and well.--A. Bronson Alcott

The mind will quote whether the tongue does or not.--Emerson

The wisdom of the wise and the experience of ages may be preserved by quotation.--Disraeli

To select well among old things is almost equal to inventing new ones.--Abbe Trublet

Let the writer's thought so ripen in thee that it becomes, as it were, thy own thought.--Chu-hi

It has been said that death ends all things. This is a mistake. It does not end the volume of practical quotations, and it will not until the sequence of the alphabet is so materially changed as to place D where Z now stands.--Harper's Bazaar

A good saying often runs the risk of being thrown away when quoted as the speaker's own.--La Bruyere

There is no less invention in aptly applying a thought found in a book, than in being the first author of the thought.--Bayle

Every book is a quotation, and every house is a quotation out of all forests and mines and stone-quarries, and every man is a quotation from all his ancestors.--Emerson

When we would prepare the mind by a forcible appeal, an opening quotation is a symphony preluding on the chords those tones we are about to harmonize.--Disraeli

He that borrows the aid of an equal understanding doubles his own; he that uses that of a superior elevates his own to the stature of that he contemplates.--Burke

All minds quote. Old and new make the warp and woof of every moment. There is no thread that is not a twist of these two strands.***We quote not only books and proverbs, but art, sciences, religion, customs, and laws; nay, we quote temples and houses, tables and chairs, by imitation.***--Emerson

Quotation, sir, is a good thing; there is a community of mind in it: classical quotation is the parole of literary men all over the world. --Johnson

An apt quotation is as good as an original remark.--Proverb

Quotation is the highest compliment you can pay to an author. --Johnson

Whatever we may say against collections, which present authors is a disjointed form, they nevertheless bring about many excellent results. We are not always so composed, so full of wisdom, that we are able to take in at once the whole scope of a work according to its merits. Do we not mark in a book passages which seem to have a direct reference to ourselves? Young people especially, who have failed in acquiring a complete cultivation of mind, are roused in a praiseworthy way by brilliant passages.--Goethe

Fine words! I wonder where you stole them.--Swift

The obscurest sayings of the truly great are often those which contain the germ of the profoundest and most useful truths.--Mazzini

Although quotation may, no doubt, be carried to excess, yet there is frequently as much ability in making a happy application of a thought of another writer as in its first conception.--Ramage

Selections have their justification. They serve a double object,--to introduce and to remind. They provide the unadventurous reader with the easiest way to learn a little of an author he feels he ought to know; and they recall the fruits of fuller study to the memories of those who have passed on to other fields.--Stanley Lane-Poole

A fine quotation is a diamond on the finger of a man of wit, and a pebble in the hand of a fool.--Joseph Roux

It is generally supposed that where there is no quotation, there will be found most originality. . . .The greater part of our writers, in consequence, have become so original that no one cares to imitate them and those who never quote, in return are seldom quoted.--Disraeli

TABLE OF CONTENTS

ACTION

Heaven never helps the man who will not act.--Sophocles

Action may not always bring happiness; but there is no happiness without action.--Disraeli

Our grand business is not to see what lies dimly at a distance, but to do what lies clearly at hand.--Carlyle

The actions of men are the best interpreters of their thoughts.--Locke

All our actions take their hue from the complexion of the heart, as landscapes do their variety from light.--W.T. Bacon

I have never heard anything about the resolutions of the apostles, but a great deal about their acts.--H. Mann

The more we do, the more we can do; the more busy we are, the more leisure we have.--Hazlitt

Unselfish and noble actions are the most radiant pages in the biography of souls.--Thomas

We must be doing something to be happy.--Action is no less necessary to us than thought.--Hazlitt

Action is eloquence; the eyes of the ignorant are more learned than their ears.--Shakespeare

ADVERSITY

No man is more unhappy than the one who is never in adversity; the greatest affliction of life is never to be afflicted.--Anon.

Adversity has ever been considered the state in which a man most easily becomes acquainted with himself, then, especially, being free from flatterers.--Johnson

Stars may be seen from the bottom of a deep well, when they cannot be discerned from the top of a mountain. So are many things learned in adversity which the prosperous man dreams not of.--Spurgeon

Prosperity has this property: It puffs up narrow souls, makes them imagine themselves high and mighty, and leads them to look down upon the world with contempt; but a truly noble spirit appears greatest in distress; and then becomes more bright and conspicuous.--Plutarch

Prosperity is a great teacher; adversity is a greater. Possession pampers the mind; privation trains and strengthens it.--Hazlitt

The brightest crowns that are worn in heaven have been tried, and smelted, and polished, and glorified through the furnace of tribulation.--E.H. Chapin

The real test in golf and in life is not in keeping out of the rough, but in getting out after we are in.--Rev. Moore

AGE

That man never grows old who keeps a child in his heart.--Anon.

Though I look old, yet I am strong and lusty; for in my youth I never did apply hot and rebellious liquors in my blood; and did not, with unbashful forehead, woo the means of weakness and debility: therefore my age is as a lusty winter, frosty but kindly.--Shakespeare

There are two things which grow stronger in the breast of man, in proportion as he advances in years; the love of country and religion. Let them be never so much forgotten in youth, they sooner or later present themselves to us arrayed in all the charms, and excite in the recesses of our hearts an attachment justly due to their beauty. --Chateaubriand

Modern civilization has little respect for the aged for the same reason it has little for tradition. There is a love for the antique but not for the ancient. Yet the aged are to culture what memory is to the mind. --Fulton Sheen

It is not by the gray of the hair that one knows the age of the heart. --Bulwer

No snow falls lighter than the snow of age; but none lies heavier, for it never melts.--Anon.

Age does not depend upon years, but upon temperament and health.--Some men are born old, and some never grow so. --T. Edwards

Nothing is more disgraceful than that an old man should have nothing to show to prove that he has lived long, except his years.--Seneca

Every one desires to live long, but no one would be old.--Swift

Old age is a blessed time. It gives us leisure to put off our earthly garments one by one, and dress ourselves for heaven. 'Blessed are they that are homesick, for they shall get home.'--R. Palmer

It is a rare and difficult attainment to grow old gracefully and happily.--Child

Age does not make us childish, as some say; it finds us true children. --Goethe

As winter strips the leaves from around us, so that we may see the distant regions they formerly concealed, so old age takes away our enjoyments only to enlarge the prospect of the coming eternity. --Richter.

It is only necessary to grow old to become more charitable and even indulgent.--I see no fault committed by others that I have not committed myself.--Goethe

When we are out of sympathy with the young, then I think our work in this world is over.--G. MacDonald

Some men never seem to grow old. Always active in thought, always ready to adopt new ideas, they are never chargeable with fogyism. Satisfied, yet ever dissatisfied, settled, yet ever unsettled, they always enjoy the best of what will be.--Anon.

AGNOSTICISM

The term "agnostic" is only the Greek equivalent of the Latin and English "Ignoramus"--A name one would think scientists would be slow to apply to themselves.--Anon.

Agnosticism is not an intellectual position, but a moral position, or better still, an intellectual defense for a life which is afraid of the light.--Fulton Sheen

Agnosticism is not always the deplorable thing it is imagined to be. An acknowledged intellectual agnosticism is a healthy thing; the difficulty arises when agnosticism is not acknowledged. To be an agnostic means I recognize that there is more than I know, and that if I am ever to know more, it must be by revelation.--Oswald Chambers

There is only one greater folly than that of the fool who says in his heart there is no God, and that is the folly of the people that says with its head that is does not know whether there is a God or not. --Bismarck

An agnostic is a man who doesn't know whether there is a God or not, doesn't know whether he has a soul or not, doesn't know whether there is a future life or not, doesn't believe that any one else knows any more about these matters than he does, and thinks it a waste of time to try to find out.--Dana

AIMS & AMBITIONS

High aims form high characters, and great objects bring out great minds.--T. Edwards

Have a purpose in life, and having it, throw into your work such strength of mind and muscle as God has given you.--Carlyle

Not failure, but low aim, is crime.--Lowell

Aim at perfection in everything, though in most things it is unattainable; however, they who aim at it, and persevere, will come much nearer to it, than those whose laziness and despondency make them give it up as unattainable.--Chesterfield.

Aim at the sun, and you may not reach it; but your arrow will fly far higher than if aimed at an object on a level with yourself.--J. Hawes

Resolved to live with all my might while I do live, and as I shall wish I had done ten thousand ages hence.--J. Edwards.

In our natural life our ambitions are our own. In the Christian life we have no aim of our own, and God's aim looks like missing the mark because we are too short sighted to see what He is aiming at. --Oswald Chambers

Dream manfully and nobly, and thy dreams shall be prophets. --Bulwer-Lytton

What are the aims which are at the same time duties?--they are the perfecting of ourselves, and the happiness of others.--Kent

ANCESTRY

The happiest lot for a man, as far as birth is concerned, is that it should be such as to give him but little occasion to think much about it.--Whately

It is of no consequence of what parents a man is born, so he be a man of merit.--Horac

Every man is his own ancestor, and every man is his own heir. He devises his own future, and he inherits his own past.--H.F. Hedge

How poor are all hereditary honors, those poor possessions from another's deeds, unless our own just virtues form our title, and give a sanction to our fond assumption.--Shirley

The origin of all mankind was the same: it is only a clear and a good conscience that makes a man noble, for that is derived from heaven itself.--Seneca

Mere family never made a man great.--Thought and deed, not pedigree, are the passports to enduring fame.--Skobeleff

Few people disparage a distinguished ancestry except those who have none of their own.--J. Hawes

Philosophy does not regard pedigree.--She did not receive Plato as a noble, but made him so.--Seneca

They who depend on the merits of ancestors, search in the roots of the tree for the fruits which the branches ought to produce.--Barrow

23

Nothing is more disgraceful than for a man who is nothing, to hold himself honored on account of his forefathers; and yet hereditary honors are a noble and splendid treasure to descendants.--Plato

The man who has nothing to boast of but his illustrious ancestry, is like the potato--the best part under grounds.--Overbury

All history shows the power of blood over circumstances, as agriculture show the power of the seeds over the soil.--Whipple

The sins of the fathers are not visited on innocent children, but on children who continue the sins of their fathers. Distinction must be made between punishment and suffering, they are not synonymous terms. A bad man's relation to his children is in God's hand: the child's relation to the badness of his father is in his own hand. Because we see children suffering physically for the sins of their parents, we say they are being punished; they are not, there is no element of punishment in their suffering; there are Divine compensations we know nothing about. The whole subject of heredity and what is transmitted by heredity, if taken out of its Bible setting, can be made the greatest slander against God, as well as the greatest exoneration of the bitterness of a man's spirit.--Oswald Chambers

We inherit nothing truly, but what our actions make us worthy of. --Chapman

APPRECIATION

Next to excellence is the appreciation of it.--Thackeray

We must never undervalue any person.--The workman loves not to have his work despised in his presence. Now God is present everywhere, and every person is his work.--De Sales

Contemporaries appreciate the man rather than the merit; but posterity will regard the merit rather than the man.--Colton

When a nation gives birth to a man who is able to produce a great thought, another is born who is able to understand and admire it. --Joubert

To love one that is great, is almost to be great one's self.--Mad. Neckar

Every man is valued in this world as he shows by his conduct that he wishes to be valued.--Bruyere

To feel exquisitely is the lot of very many; but to appreciate belongs to the few.--Only one or two, here and there, have the blended passion and understanding which, in its essence, constitute worship.--C. Auchester

We are very much what others think of us.--The reception our observations meet with gives us courage to proceed, or damps our efforts. --Hazlitt

He is incapable of a truly good action who finds not a pleasure in contemplating the good actions of others.--Lavater

ASPIRATION

To get anywhere worthwhile, one must take a ticket of preparation, and get on the tracks of heart-effort and hammer and tongs, thick and thin endeavor.--John Wanamaker

It is not for man to rest in absolute contentment.--He is born to hopes and aspirations as the sparks fly upward, unless he has brutified his nature and quenched the spirit of immortality which is his portion.-- Southey

They build too low who build beneath the skies.--Young

Be always displeased with what thou art if thou desire to attain to what thou art not, for where thou hast pleased thyself, there thou abidest.--Quarles

What we truly and earnestly aspire to be, that in some sense we are. The mere aspiration, by changing the frame of the mind, for the moment realizes itself.--Mrs. Jameson

To wish is of little account; to succeed you must earnestly desire, and this desire must shorten thy sleep.--Ovid

You will become as small as your controlling desire; as great as your dominant aspiration.--James Allen

Our aspirations are our possibilities.--Robert Browning

ASSOCIATES

Tell me with whom thou art found, and I will tell thee who thou art.
--Goethe

If you wish to be held in esteem, you must associate only with those
who are estimable.--Bruyere

In all societies it is advisable to associate if possible with the highest;
not that they are always the best, but because, if disgusted there, we
can always descend; but if we begin with the lowest to ascend is
impossible.--Colton

We gain nothing by being with such as ourselves; we encourage each
other in mediocrity.--I am always longing to be with men more excellent than myself.--Lamb

You may depend upon it that he is a good man whose intimate
friends are all good, and whose enemies are decidedly bad.--Lavater

A man should live with his superiors as he does with his fire: not too
near, lest he burn; nor too far off, lest he freeze.--Diogenes

It is best to be with those in time, that we hope to be with in eternity.--Fuller

It is certain that either wise bearing or ignorant carriage is caught, as
men take diseases, one of another; therefore let men take heed of their
company.--Shakespeare

When one associates with vice, it is but one step from companionship
to slavery.--Quarles

There is no man who has not some interesting associations with particular scenes, or airs, or books, and who does not feel their beauty or
sublimity enhanced to him by such connections.--Alison

Be cautious with whom you associate, and never give your company
or your confidence to those of whose good principles you are not
sure.--Bp. Coleridge

Successful businessmen are found associating with other successful businessmen at their clubs and social gatherings. In other words, water seeks its own level.--Dr. Paul Parker

You are the same today as you'll be in five years except for two things, the people you meet and the books you read.--Anon.

Associate with men of judgment, for judgment is found in conversation, and we make another man's judgment ours by frequenting his company.--Thomas Fuller

Company, villainous company hath been the ruin of me. --Shakespeare

Associate with people that are doing things, others steal your time.-- Simmons

ATHEISM

To be an atheist requires an infinitely greater measure of faith than to receive all the great truths which atheism would deny.--Addison

Few men are so obstinate in their atheism, that a pressing danger will not compel them to the acknowledgement of a divine power.--Plato

A little philosophy inclineth men's minds to atheism; but depth in philosophy bringeth men's minds to religion; for while the mind of man looketh upon second causes scattered, it may sometimes rest in them, and go no further.--But when it beholdeth the chain of them, confederate and linked together, it must needs fly to Providence and Deity.--Bacon

. . .the modern atheist is always angered when he hears anything said about God and religion--he would be incapable of such a resentment if God were only a myth.--Fulton Sheen

Atheism is a disease of the soul, before it becomes an error of the understanding.--Plato

Atheists put on a false courage in the midst of their darkness and misapprehensions, like children who when they fear to go in the dark, will sing or whistle to keep up their courage.--Pope

What can be more foolish than to think that all this rare fabric of heaven and earth could come by chance, when all the skill of art is not able to make an oyster? To see rare effects, and no cause; a motion, without a mover; a circle, without a centre; a time, without an eternity; a second, without a first: these are things so against philosophy and natural reason, that he must be a beast in understanding who can believe in them. The thing formed, says that nothing formed it; and that which is made, is, while that which made it is not! This is folly in infinite.--Jeremy Taylor

God never wrought miracles to convince atheism, because His ordinary works convince it.--Bacon

Atheism has moved from the intellectual plane, where it was in the last century, to the existential plane; from the level of proving atheism to the living it; from the nonexistence of God to the existence of humanity. Atheism posts a new god, namely, Man.--Oswald Chambers

Whoever considers the study of anatomy can never be an atheist. --Lord Herbert.

BIBLE

. . .we find the Bible difficult because we try to read it as we would read any other book, and it is not the same as any other book.--A.B. Tozer

There never was found, in any age of the world, either religion or law that did so highly exalt the public good as the Bible.--Bacon

The Scriptures teach us the best way of living, the noblest way of suffering, and the most comfortable way of dying.--Flavel

There are no songs comparable to the songs of Zion; no orations equal to those of the prophets; and no politics like those which the Scriptures teach.--Milton

If the Bible agreed with modern science, it would soon be out of date, because, in the very nature of things, modern science is bound to change.--Oswald Chambers

It is a belief in the Bible, the fruit of deep meditation, which has served me as the guide of my moral and literary life.--I have found it a capital safely invested, and richly productive of interest.--Goethe

The longer you read the Bible, the more you will like it; it will grow sweeter and sweeter; and the more you get into the spirit of it, the more you will get into the spirit of Christ.--Romaine

I have always said, I always will say, that the studious perusal of the sacred volume will make better citizens, better fathers, and better husbands.--Jefferson

There is only one thing better than memorizing scripture; realizing it.--C.E. Jones

We account the Scriptures of God to be the most sublime philosophy. I find more sure marks of authenticity in the Bible than in any profane history whatever.--Issac Newton

Hold fast to the Bible as the sheet-anchor of your liberties; write its precepts in your hearts, and practice them in your lives. To the influence of this book we are indebted for all the progress made in true civilization, and to this we must look as our guide in the future. 'Righteousness exalteth a nation; but sin is a reproach to any people.'--U.S. Grant

The most learned, acute, and diligent student cannot, in the longest life, obtain an entire knowledge of this one volume. The more deeply he works the mine, the richer and more abundant he finds the ore; new light continually beams from this source of heavenly knowledge, to direct the conduct, and illustrate the work of God and the ways of man; and he will at last leave the world confessing, that the more he studied the Scriptures, the fuller conviction he had of his own ignorance, and of their inestimable value.--Walter Scott

A noble book! All men's book! It is our first, oldest statement of the neverending problem,--man's destiny and God's ways with him here on earth; and all in its sincerity; in its simplicity and its epic melody. --Carlyle

No lawyer can afford to be ignorant of the Bible.--Rufus Choate

It is impossible to mentally or socially enslave a Bible-reading people. The principles of the Bible are the groundwork of human freedom. --Horace Greeley

Voltaire spoke of the Bible as a shortlived book. He said that within a hundred years it would pass from common use. Not many people read Voltaire today, but his house has been packed with Bibles as a depot of a Bible society.--Bruce Barton

The man of one book is always formidable; but when that book is the Bible he is irresistible.--W.M. Taylor

The Bible is one of the greatest blessings bestowed by God on the children of men.--It has God for its author; salvation for its end, and truth without any mixture for its matter.--It is all pure, all sincere; nothing too much; nothing wanting.--Locke

Some believe and some do not; some are morally receptive and some are not; some have spiritual capacity and some have not. It is to those who do and are and have that the Bible is addressed. Those who do not and are not and have not will read it in vain.--A.W. Tozer

I cannot too greatly emphasize the importance and value of Bible study--more important than ever before in these days of uncertainties, when men and women are apt to decide questions from the stand-point of expediency rather than on the eternal principles laid down by God, Himself.--John Wanamaker

I believe a knowledge of the Bible without a college course is more valuable than a college course without a Bible.--W.L. Phelps

All that I am I owe to Jesus Christ, revealed to me in His divine Book. --David Livingstone

To my early knowledge of the Bible I owe the best part of my taste in literature, and the most precious, and on the whole, the one essential part of my education.--Ruskin

I know the Bible is inspired because it finds me at greater depths of my being than any other book.--Coleridge

I believe that the Bible is to be understood and received in the plain and obvious meaning of its passages; for I cannot persuade myself that a book intended for the instruction and conversion of the whole world should cover its true meaning in any such mystery and doubt that none but critics and philosophers can discover it.--Webster

The Gospel is not merely a book--it is a living power--a book surpassing all others.--I never omit to read it, and every day with the same pleasure. Nowhere is to be found such a series of beautiful ideas, and admirable moral maxims, which pass before us like the battalions of a celestial army. . .The soul can never go astray with this book for its guide.--Napoleon on St. Helena

Nobody ever outgrows Scripture; the book widens and deepens with our years.--Spurgeon

There is no book on which we can rest in a dying moment but the Bible.--Selden

Holy Scripture is a stream of running water, where alike the elephant may swim, and the lamb walk without losing its feet.--Gregory the Great

A loving trust in the Author of the Bible is the best preparation for a wise and profitable study of the Bible itself.--H.C. Trumbull

Just as all things upon earth represent and image forth all the realities of another world, so the Bible is one mighty representative of the whole spiritual life of humanity.--Helen Keller

A Bible and a newspaper in every house, a good school in every district--all studied and appreciated as they merit--are the principal support of virtue, morality, and civil liberty.--Franklin

All human discoveries seem to be made only for the purpose of confirming more and more strongly the truths that come from on high and are contained in the sacred writings.--Herschel

Read some of the Bible every day. It could save your life. The Bible is accurate! If the Bible tells where there is a source of water, the chances are great that it will still be there.--General George Patton

BIOGRAPHY

A man's biography is written in terms not so much of what he causes to happen, but rather what happens *to* him and *in* him. The difference between men is not in the adversity which comes to them, but rather how they meet the adversity.--Fulton Sheen

The best teachers of humanity are the lives of great men.--Fowler

To be ignorant of the lives of the most celebrated men of antiquity is to continue in a state of childhood all our days.--Plutarch

Biography, especially of the great and good, who have risen by their own exertions to eminence and usefulness, is an inspiring and ennobling study.--Its direct tendency is to reproduce the excellence it records.--H. Mann

A life that is worth writing at all, is worth writing minutely and truthfully.--Longfellow

Biographies of great, but especially of good men, are most instructive and useful as helps, guides, and incentives to others. Some of the best are almost equivalent to gospels--teaching high living, high thinking, and energetic actions for their own and the world's good. --S. Smiles

There is properly no history, only biography.--Emerson

Biography is the most universally pleasant and profitable of all reading.--Carlyle

BOOKS

The books and the men who help us most are not those who teach us, but those who can express for us what we feel inarticulate about. --Oswald Chambers

A book is the only immortality.--R. Choate

Books are lighthouses erected in the great sea of time.--E.P. Whipple

Books are embalmed minds.--Bovee

A good book is the very essence of a good man.--His virtues survive in it, while the foibles and faults of his actual life are forgotten.--All the goodly company of the excellent and great sit around my table or look down on me from yonder shelves, waiting patiently to answer my questions and enrich me with their wisdom.--A precious book is a foretaste of immortality.--T.L. Cuyler

Any book which inspires us to lead a better life is a good book. --Fulton Sheen

I love to lose myself in other men's minds. When I am not walking, I am reading. I cannot sit and think; books think for me.--Charles Lamb

Books are masters who instruct us without rods or ferrules, without words or anger, without bread or money. If you approach them, they are not asleep; if you seek them, they do not hide; if you blunder, they do not scold; if you are ignorant, they do not laugh at you.--Richard de Bury

God be thanked for books; they are the voices of the distant and the dead, and make us heirs of the spiritual life of past ages.--Channing

If a book comes from the heart it will contrive to reach other hearts. --All art and authorcraft are of small account to that.--Carlyle

Some books are to be tasted; others swallowed; and some few to be chewed and digested.--Bacon

Except a living man there is nothing more wonderful than a book! A message to us from the dead--from human souls we never saw, who lived, perhaps, thousands of miles away. And yet these, in those little sheets of paper, speak to us, arouse us, terrify us, teach us, comfort us, open their hearts to us as brothers.--Charles Kingsley

Books are the most wonderful friends in the world. When you meet them and pick them up, they are always ready to give you a few ideas. When you put them down, they never get mad; when you take them up again, they seem to enrich you all the more.--Fulton Sheen

Books are those faithful mirrors that reflect to our mind the minds of sages and heroes.--Gibbon

A good book is the precious life-blood of a master-spirit, embalmed and treasured up on purpose for a life beyond.--Milton

Books, like friends, should be few and well chosen. Like friends, too, we should return to them again and again--For, like true friends, they will never fail us--never cease to instruct--never cloy--Next to acquiring good friends, the best acquisition is that of good books.--Colton

Without books, God is silent, justice dormant, natural science at a stand, philosophy lame, letters dumb, and all things involved in darkness.--Bartholini

Books are the legacies that genius leaves to mankind, to be delivered down from generation to generation, as presents to those that are yet unborn.--Addison

If all the crowns of Europe were placed at my disposal on condition that I should abandon my books and studies, I should spurn the crowns away and stand by the books.--Fenelon

Books are immortal sons deifying their sires.--Plato

When I get a little money, I buy books; and if any is left, I buy food and clothes.--Erasmus

Books are a guide in youth, and an entertainment for age. They support us under solitude, and keep us from becoming a burden to ourselves. They help us to forget the crossness of men and things, compose our cares and our passions, and lay our disappointments asleep. When we are weary of the living, we may repair to the dead, who have nothing of peevishness, pride, or design in their conversation. --Jeremy Collier

Every man is a volume if you know how to read him.--Channing

A house without books is like a room without windows. No man has a right to bring up his children without surrounding them with books, if he has the means to buy them. It is a wrong to his family. Children learn to read by being in the presence of books. The love of knowledge comes with reading and grows upon it. And the love of knowledge, in a young mind, is almost a warrant against the inferior excitement of passions and vices.--H. Mann

A good book is the best of friends, the same today and forever. --Tupper

The books that help you most, are those which make you think the most.--The hardest way of learning is that of easy reading; but a great book that comes from a great thinker is a ship of thought, deep freighted with truth and beauty.--Theodore Parker

The best of a book is not the thought which it contains, but the thought which it suggests; just as the charm of music dwells not in the tones but in the echoes of our hearts.--O.W. Holmes

That is a good book which is opened with expectation, and closed with delight and profit.--A.B. Alcott

The society of dead authors has this advantage over that of the living; they never flatter us to our faces, nor slander us behind our backs, nor intrude upon our privacy, nor quit their shelves until we take them down.--Colton

When a new book comes out I read an old one.--Rogers

No book can be so good as to be profitable when negligently read. --Seneca

If religious books are not widely circulated among the masses in this country, and the people do not become religious, I do not know what is to become of us as a nation. And the thought is one to cause solemn reflection on the part of every patriot and Christian. If truth be not diffused, error will be; if God, and His word are not known and received, the devil and his works will gain the ascendancy; if the evangelical volume does not reach every hamlet, the pages of a corrupt and licentious literature will; if the power of the gospel is not felt through the length and breadth of the land, anarchy and misrule, degradation and misery, corruption and darkness, will reign without mitigation or end.--Daniel Webster

To use books rightly, is to go to them for help; to appeal to them when our own knowledge and power fail; to be led by them into wider sight and purer conception than our own, and to receive from them the united sentence of the judges and councils of all time, against our solitary and unstable opinions.--Ruskin

Books are the true levellers.--They give to all who faithfully use them, the society, the spiritual presence of the greatest and best of our race.--Channing

The book to read is not the one which thinks for you, but the one which makes you think. No book in the world equals the Bible for that.--McCosh

The most foolish kind of a book is a kind of leaky boat on the sea of wisdom; some of the wisdom will get in anyhow.--O.W. Holmes

Master books, but do not let them master you.--Read to live, not live to read.--Bulwer-Lytton

Books are the best of things if well used; if abused, among the worst. --They are good for nothing but to inspire.--I had better never see a book than be warped by its attraction clean out of my own orbit, and made a satellite instead of a system.--Emerson

Many books require no thought from those who read them, and for a very simple reason; they made no such demand upon those who wrote them. Those works, therefore, are the most valuable, that set our thinking faculties in the fullest operation.--Colton

A book is a garden, an orchard, a storehouse, a party, a company by the way, a counselor, a multitude of counselors.--H. W. Beecher

Most books, like their authors, are born to die; of only a few books can it be said that death hath no dominion over them; they live, and their influence lives forever.--J. Swartz

We ought to reverence books; to look on them as useful and mighty things.--If they are good and true, whether they are about religion, politics, farming, trade, law, or medicine, they are the message of Christ, the maker of all things--the teacher of all truth.--C. Kingsley

CHARACTER

The one thing God is after is character.--Oswald Chambers

Not education, but character, is man's greatest need and man's greatest safeguard.--Spencer

I cannot hold other people's tongues, and it has taken me a long time to get control of my own tongue. But it can be done, and it is well worth while. If for no other reason, it saves a lot of time!--John Wanamaker

Talents are best nurtured in solitude; character is best formed in the stormy billows of the world.--Goethe

Men best show their character in trifles, where they are not on their guard.--It is in insignificant matters, and in the boundless egotism which pays no regard to the feelings of others, and denies nothing to itself.--Schopenhauer

Character and personal force are the only investments that are worth anything.--Whitman

Characters do not change.--Opinions alter, but characters are only developed.--Disraeli

The shortest and surest way to live with honor in the world, is to be in reality what we would appear to be; all human virtues increase and strengthen themselves by the practice and experience of them. --Socrates

Our character is but the stamp on our souls of the free choices of good and evil we have made through life.--Geikie

Truthfulness is a corner-stone in character, and if it be not firmly laid in youth, there will ever after be a weak spot in the foundation.--J. Davis

Character is the result of two things: Mental attitude and the way we spend our time.--Elbert Hubbard

The miracle, or the power, that elevates the few is to be found in their industry, application, and perseverance under the promptings of a brave, determined spirit.--Mark Twain

If you would create something, you must be something.--Goethe

No amount of ability is of the slightest avail without honor.--Andrew Carnegie

If I take care of my character, my reputation will take care of itself.
--D.L. Moody

Character is higher than intellect. . .A great soul will be strong to live
as well to think.--Emerson

. . .a crisis does not make character; a crisis reveals character.--Oswald
Chambers

The great thing in this world is not so much where we are, but in
what direction we are moving.--O.W. Holmes

Never does a man portray his own character more vividly, than in his
manner of portraying another.--Richter

CHEERFULNESS

The highest wisdom is continual cheerfulness; such a state, like the
region about the moon, is always clear and serene.--Montaigne

Wondrous is the strength of cheerfulness, and its power of
endurance--the cheerful man will do more in the same time, will do
it better, will persevere in it longer, than the sad or sullen.--Carlyle

Honest good humor is the oil and wine of a merry meeting, and there
is no jovial companionship equal to that where the jokes are rather
small and the laughter abundant.--Washington Irving

Cheerfulness is as natural to the heart of a man in strong health, as
color to his cheek; and wherever there is habitual gloom, there must
be either bad air, unwholesome food, improperly severe labor, or
erring habits of life.--Ruskin

Get into the habit of looking for the silver lining of the cloud, and,
when you have found it, continue to look at it, rather than at the lead-
en gray in the middle. It will help you over many hard places.
--Wilitts

Wondrous is the strength of cheerfulness, altogether past calculation
its powers of endurance. Efforts, to be permanently useful, must be
uniformly joyous,--a spirit all sunshine, graceful from very gladness,
beautiful because bright.--Carlyle

To be free-minded and cheerfully disposed at hours of meals, and of sleep, and of exercise, is one of the best precepts of long-lasting. --Bacon

Cheerfulness is health; its opposite, melancholy, is disease. --Haliburton

The true source of cheerfulness is benevolence.--The soul that perpetually overflows with kindness and sympathy will always be cheerful.--P. Godwin

The mind that is cheerful at present will have no solicitude for the future, and will meet the bitter occurrences of life with a smile. --Horace

To make knowledge valuable, you must have the cheerfulness of wisdom. Goodness smiles to the last.--Emerson

There is no greater every-day virtue than cheerfulness. This quality in man among men is like sunshine to the day, or gentle renewing moisture to parched herbs. The light of a cheerful face diffuses itself, and communicates the happy spirit that inspires it. The sourest temper must sweeten in the atmosphere of continuous good humor. A light heart lives long.--Shakespeare

Every one must have felt that a cheerful friend is like a sunny day, which sheds its brightness on all around; and most of us can, as we choose, make of this world either a palace or a prison.--Sir J. Lubbock

CHILDREN

Children have more need of models than of critics.--Joubert

Profoundly speaking, a child is not pure, and yet the innocence of a child charms us because it makes visible all that we understand by purity.--Chambers

Blessed be the hand that prepares a pleasure for a child, for there is no saying when and where it may bloom forth.--Jerrold.

You save an old man and you save a unit; but save a boy and you save a multiplication table.--"Gipsy" Smith

You cannot teach a child to take care of himself unless you will let him try to take care of himself. He will make mistakes; and out of these mistakes will come his wisdom.--H.W. Beecher

An infallible way to make your child miserable, is to satisfy all his demands.--Passion swells by gratification; and the impossibility of satisfying every one of his wishes will oblige you to stop short at last after he has become headstrong.--Home

Children generally hate to be idle.--All the care then should be, that their busy humor should be constantly employed in something that is of use to them.--Locke

The first duty to children is to make them happy.--If you have not made them so, you have wronged them.--No other good they may get can make up for that.--Buxton

The child's heart curseth deeper in the silence than the strong man in his wrath.--E.B. Browning

What the best and wisest parent wants for his own child that must the community want for all its children.--John Dewey

The root of this trouble is in the *home;* and those who talk about more nurseries, better playgrounds, curfews, better milk, and more dance halls, are perhaps diminishing the effect but not removing the cause. --Fulton Sheen

The only way on God's earth you will ever solve the problem of reaching the masses, is by getting hold of the Children. You get boys and girls started right and the devil will hang crepe on his door. --Billy Sunday

. . .If I never correct my child I am making a nice mess for other folks by and by.--Oswald Chambers

Above all things endeavor to breed them up in the love of virtue, and that holy plain way of it which we have lived in, that the world in no part of it get into my family. I had rather they were homely, than finely bread as to outward behavior; yet I love sweetness mixed with gravity, and cheerfulness tempered with sobriety.--Penn to his wife

The true idea of self-restraint is to let a child venture.--The mistakes of children are often better than their no-mistakes.--H.W. Beecher

CONFIDENCE

Confidence! Confidence! Confidence! That is your capital.--John Wanamaker

Fields are won by those who believe in winning.--T.W. Higginson

I think I have learned, in some degree at least, to disregard the old maxim, "Do not let others to do what you can do yourself." My motto on the other hand is, "Do not do that which others can do as well."--Booker T. Washington

A great point is reached spiritually when we stop worrying God over personal matters or over any matter. God expects of us the one thing that glorifies Him--and that is to remain absolutely confident in Him, remembering what He has said beforehand, and sure that His purpose will be fulfilled.--Oswald Chambers

Trust men and they will be true to you; treat them greatly and they will show themselves great.--Emerson

They can conquer who believe they can.--Dryden

Confidence imparts a wondrous inspiration to its possessor.--It bears him on in security, either to meet no danger, or to find matter of glorious trial.--Milton

"I can do all things through Christ which strengtheneth me." The man who believes this has calm, quiet, confidence, but, because his confidence is based upon God's power and not his own power, there is never the slightest speck of egotism.--Clinton Davidson

CONTENTMENT

If you are but content you have enough to live upon with comfort. --Plautus

I am always content with what happens; for I know that what God chooses is better than what I choose.--Epictetus

If two angels were sent down from heaven, one to conduct an empire, and the other to sweep a street, they would feel no inclination to change employments.--John Newton

To be content with even the best people, we must be contented with little and bear a great deal. Those who are most perfect have many imperfections, and we have great faults; between the two, mutual toleration becomes very difficult.--Fenelon

True contentment depends not upon what we have; a tub was large enough for Diogenes, but a world was too little for Alexander. --Colton

A man who finds no satisfaction in himself, seeks for it in vain elsewhere.--Rochenfoucauld

Learn to be pleased with everything; with wealth, so far as it makes us beneficial to others; with poverty, for not having much to care for; and with obscurity, for being unenvied.--Plutarch

Contentment is natural wealth, luxury is artificial poverty.--Socrates

CONVERSATION

It is good to rub and polish our brain against that of others. --Montaigne

The first ingredient in conversation is truth; the next, good sense; the third, good humor; and the fourth, wit.--Sir W. Temple

Know how to listen, and you will profit even from those who talk badly.--Plutarch

Good talk is like good scenery--continuous, yet constantly varying, and full of the charm of novelty and surprise.--Randolph S. Bourne

I don't like to talk much with people who always agree with me. It is amusing to coquette with an echo for a little while, but one soon tires of it.--Carlyle

Silence is one great art of conversation.--Hazlitt

As it is the characteristic of great wits to say much in few words, so it is of small wits to talk much, and say nothing.--Rochefoucauld

Not only to say the right thing in the right place, but far more difficult, to leave unsaid the wrong thing at the tempting moment.--Sala

All bitter feelings are avoided, or at least greatly reduced by prompt, face-to-face discussion.--Walter B. Pitkin

One of the best rules in conversation is, never to say a thing which any of the company can reasonably wish had been left unsaid.--Swift

Be sincere. Be simple in words, manners and gestures. Amuse as well as instruct. If you can make a man laugh, you can make him think and make him like and believe you.--Alfred E. Smith

My observation is that, generally speaking, poverty of speech is the outward evidence of poverty of mind.--Bruce Barton

For good or ill, your conversation is your advertisement. Every time you open your mouth you let men look into your mind. Do they see it well clothed, neat, businesslike?--Bruce Barton

Patrick Henry was more impressed by Washington's quiet conversation than by the fervid oratory of others. When asked whom he considered the greatest man in congress, he answered: "Rutledge, if you speak of eloquence, is by far the greatest orator, but Colonel Washington, who has no pretensions to eloquence, is a man of more solid judgment and information than any man on that floor."--Rupert Hughes

Conversation should be pleasant without scurrility, witty without affectation, free without indecency, learned without conceitedness, novel without falsehood.--Shakespeare

We sometimes disputed, and very fond we were of argument, and very desirous of confuting one another, which is apt to become a very bad habit. I had caught it by reading my father's books of dispute about religion. Persons of good sense, I have since observed, seldom fall into it, except lawyers, university men, and men of all sorts that have been bred at Edinburgh.--Benjamin Franklin

43

A single conversation across the table with a wise man is worth a month's study of books.--Chinese Proverb

Conversation is the laboratory and workshop of the student. --Emerson

There has never been a person who monopolized a conversation without at the same time monotonizing it.--Fulton Sheen

Conversation is an art in itself.--Lubbock

Anecdotes and maxims are rich treasures to the man of the world, for he knows how to introduce the former to fit places in conversation and to recollect the latter on proper occasion.--Goethe

COURAGE

Courage consists, not in blindly overlooking danger, but in seeing and conquering it.--Richter

Conscience is the root of all true courage; if a man would be brave let him obey his conscience.--J.F. Clarke

True courage is cool and calm.--The bravest of men have the least of a brutal, bullying insolence, and in the very time of danger are found the most serene and free.--Saftsbury

It is an error to suppose that courage means courage in everything. --Most people are brave only in the dangers to which they accustom themselves, either in imagination or practice.--Bulwer-Lytton

True courage is not the brutal force of vulgar heroes, but the firm resolve of virtue and reason.--Whitehead

True courage is the result of reasoning.--Resolution lies more in the head than in the veins; and a just sense of honor and of infamy, of duty and of religion, will carry us farther than all the force of mechanism.--Collier

Courage consists not in hazarding without fear, but being resolutely minded in a just cause.--Plutarch

DEATH

Did you ever stop to think how much more exciting death will be than life?--Gen. George Patton

This world is the land of the dying: the next is the land of the living. --Tryon Edwards

Men fear death, as if unquestionably the greatest evil, and yet no man knows that it may not be the greatest good.--W. Mitford

One may live as a conqueror, a king, or a magistrate; but he must die a man. The bed of death brings every human being to his pure individuality, to the intense contemplation of that deepest and most solemn of all relations--the relation between the creature and his Creator.--Daniel Webster

Be still prepared for death: and death or life shall thereby be the sweeter.--Shakespeare

Cullen, in his last moments, whispered, "I wish I had the power of writing or speaking, for then I would describe to you how pleasant a thing it is to die."--Derby

Living is death; dying is life.--On this side of the grave we are exiles, on that, citizens; on this side, orphans; on that, children; on this side, captives; on that, freemen; on this side disguised, unknown; on that, disclosed and proclaimed as the sons of God.--H.W. Beecher

He who should teach men to die, would, at the same time, teach them to live.--Montaigne

Death and love are the two wings that bear the good man to heaven. --M. Angelo

Let death be daily before your eyes, and you will never entertain any abject thought, nor too eagerly covet anything.--Epictetus

As long as we are living, God will give us living grace, and he won't give us dying grace till it's time to die. What's the use of trying to feel like dying when you ain't dying, nor anywhere near it?--H.W. Beecher

Death is the golden key that opens the palace of eternity.--Milton

Alexander the Great, seeing Diogenes looking attentively at a parcel of human bones, asked the philosopher what he was looking for. "That which I cannot find," was the reply; "the difference between your father's bones and those of his slaves."

A good man being asked during his last illness, whether he thought himself dying, "Really, friend, I care not whether I am or not; for if I die I shall be with God; if I live, He will be with me."--Anon.

Not by lamentations and mournful chants ought we to celebrate the funeral of a good man, but by hymns, for in ceasing to be numbered with mortals he enters upon the heritage of a diviner life.--Plutarch

A lot of people die at forty but are not buried until thirty years later. --Patton

I am the resurrection and the life.--Jesus Christ

DECISION

When a decision has to be made, make it. There is no totally right time for anything.--Gen. George Patton

There is nothing more to be esteemed than a manly firmness and decision of character.--I like a person who knows his own mind and sticks to it; who sees at once what, in given circumstances, is to be done, and does it.--Hazlitt

Decision of character will often give to an inferior mind command over a superior.--W. Wirt

All the world over it is true that a double-minded man is unstable in all his ways, like a wave on the streamlet, tossed hither and thither with every eddy of its tide.--A determinate purpose in life and a steady adhesion to it through all disadvantages, are indispensable conditions of success.--W.M. Punshon

It is a poor and disgraceful thing not to be able to reply, with some degree of certainty, to the simple questions, "What will you be? What will you do?"--John Foster

Never postpone a moral decision. Second thoughts in moral matters are always deflections. Give as many second thoughts as you like to matters of prudence, but in the presence of God never think twice. --Oswald Chambers

Men must be decided on what they will not do, and then they are able to set with vigor in what they ought to do.--Mencius

Make your decision, make it yours, and live and die by it.--C.E. Jones

Life's three greatest decisions are: Who will you live your life with?--Marriage; what will you live it in?--Work; What will you live it for?--Purpose.--C.E. Jones

DEFEAT

What is defeat?--Nothing but education; nothing but the first step to something better.--Wendell Phillips

Defeat is a school in which truth always grows strong.--H.W. Beecher

Robert E. Lee was one of America's greatest men. He was a great general, but his real greatness was shown in defeat. He accepted it without fear, hate, or rancor.--William Ross

No man is defeated without some resentment, which will be continued with obstinacy while he believes himself in the right, and asserted with bitterness, if even to his own conscience he is detected in the wrong.--Johnson

It is defeat that turns bone to flint, and gristle to muscle, and makes men invincible, and formed those heroic natures that are now in ascendency in the world.--Do not then be afraid of defeat.--You are never so near to victory as when defeated in a good cause.--H.W. Beecher

Defeat should never be a source of discouragement, but rather a fresh stimulus.--Robert South

Success is not how high did you reach, but how high did you bounce when you hit the ground.--Gen. George Patton

DISCIPLINE

The resentment of discipline of any kind will warp the whole life away from God's purpose.--Oswald Chambers

It is good to have a systematic way of doing things, but it is more important to be sure that you do them.--John Wanamaker

What happens when we get so many mean kids that the police cannot spank the kids? Self-punishment! Self-punishment is the worst type and the most severe. The kid who cannot discipline himself becomes the man who cannot control his eating and drinking--or his use of drugs. What's the punishment? Liver failure, all kinds of heart problems, lung cancer, and many other severe punishments are given by Mother Nature and God. Could be years later.--Gen. George Patton

A man in old age is like a sword in a shop window.--Men that look upon the perfect blade do not imagine the process by which it was completed.--Man is a sword; daily life is the workshop; and God is the artificer; and those cares which beat upon the anvil, and file the edge, and eat in, acid-like, the inscription on the hilt--those are the very things that fashion the man.--H.W. Beecher

A stern discipline pervades all nature, which is a little cure that may be very kind.--Spenser

No pain, no palm; no thorns, no throne; no gall, no glory; no cross, no crown.--Penn

DRESS

Any man out of uniform or with long hair and dirt stays on the post. No man can have any pride if he looks as if he has to go to the bathroom or has just been there!--Gen. George Patton

Dress has a moral effect upon the conduct of mankind.--Let any gentleman find himself with dirty boots, old surtout, soiled neckcloth, and a general negligence of dress, and he will, in all probability, find a corresponding disposition in negligence of address.--Sir J. Barrington

As you treat your body, so your house, your domestics, your enemies, your friends.--Dress is the table of your contents.--Lavater

The body is the shell of the soul, and dress the husk of that shell; but the husk often tells what the kernel is.--Anon

Eat to please thyself, but dress to please others.--Franklin

Costly thy habit as thy purse can buy, but not expressed in fancy; rich, but not gaudy, for the apparel oft proclaims the man.
--Shakespeare

A gentleman's taste in dress is, upon principle, the avoidance of all things extravagant.--It consists in the quiet simplicity of exquisite neatness; but as the neatness must be a neatness in fashion, employ the best tailor; pay him ready money; and on the whole you will find him the cheapest.--Bulwer

Had Cicero himself pronounced one of his orations with a blanket about his shoulders, more people would have laughed at his dress than admired his eloquence.--Addison

As to matters of dress, I would recommend one never to be first in the fashion nor the last out of it.--J. Wesley

An emperor in his night-cap would not meet with half the respect of an emperor with a crown.--Goldsmith

Dress yourself fine, where others are fine, and plain, where others are plain; but take care always that your clothes are well made and fit you, for otherwise they will give you a very awkward air.
--Chesterfield

In civilized society external advantages make us more respected.--A man with a good coat on his back meets with a better reception than he who has a bad one.--You may analyze this and say, what is there in it?--But that will avail you nothing, for it is a part of a general system.--Johnson

Those who think that in order to dress well it is necessary to dress extravagantly or grandly, make a great mistake.--Nothing so well becomes true feminine beauty as simplicity.--G.D. Prentice

The only medicine which does women more good than harm, is dress.--Richter

DRUNKENNESS

Drunkenness is nothing else but a voluntary madness.--Seneca

There are two ways of inspiration possible--being drunk with wine, and being filled with the Spirit. We have no business to be nondescript, drunk neither one way nor the other. A man may be sober and incapable as well as drunk and incapable. Watch human nature; we are so built that if we do not get thrilled in the right way, we will get thrilled in the wrong. If we are without the thrill of communion with God, we will try to get thrilled by the devil, or by some concoction of human ingenuity.--Chambers

Intoxicating drinks have produced evils more deadly, because more continuous, than all those caused to mankind by the great historic scourges of war, famine, and pestilence combined.--Gladstone

Some of the domestic evils of drunkenness are houses without windows, gardens without fences, fields without tillage, barns without roofs, children without clothing, principles, morals, or manners. --Franklin

What is a drunken man like? Like a drown'd man, a fool, and a madman; one draught above heat makes him a fool; the second mads him; and a third drowns him.--Shakespeare

All the armies on earth do not destroy so many of the human race, nor alienate so much property, as drunkenness.--Bacon

DUTY

Everyone honors the man who fulfills a duty at all hazards.--John Wanamaker

There is not a moment without some duty.--Cicero

We do not choose our own parts in life, and have nothing to do with selecting those parts. Our simple duty is confined to playing them well.--Epictetus

Duty is carrying on promptly and faithfully the affairs now before you.--It is to fulfill the claims of today.--Goethe

Every duty which we omit, obscures some truth which we should have known.--Ruskin

Let us never forget that every station in life is necessary; that each deserves our respect; that not the station itself, but the worthy fulfillment of its duties does honor to man.--Anon.

There is nothing in the universe that I fear, but that I shall not know all my duty, or shall fail to do it.--Mary Lyon

There is no evil we cannot face or fly from, but the consciousness of duty disregarded.--Daniel Webster

Be not diverted from your duty by any idle reflections the silly world may make upon you, for their censures are not in your power and should not be at all your concern.--Epictetus

Try to put well in practice what you already know; and in so doing, you will, in good time, discover the hidden things which you now inquire about. Practice what you know, and it will help to make clear what now you do not know.--Rembrandt

All that any one of us has to do in this world is his simple duty. And an archangel could not do more than that to advantage.--H.C. Trumbull

When the soul resolves to perform every duty, immediately it is conscious of the presence of God.--Bacon

If I am faithful to the duties of the present, God will provide for the future.--Bedell

It is wonderful what strength and boldness of purpose and energy will come from the feeling that we are in the way of duty.--John Foster

Do the truth ye know, and you shall learn the truth you need to know.--G. MacDonald

51

Do thy duty; that is best; leave unto the Lord the rest.--Longfellow

The duty of man is plain and simple, and consists but of two points; his duty to God, which every man must feel; and his duty to his neighbor, to do as he would be done by.--Thomas Paine

Do the duty that lies nearest to thee.--Goethe

EDUCATION

The great end of education is, to discipline rather than to furnish the mind; to train it to the use of its own powers, rather than fill it with the accumulations of others.--Tryon Edwards

The best education in the world is that got by struggling to get a living.--W. Philips

The aim of education should be to teach us rather how to think, than what to think--rather to improve our minds, so as to enable us to think for ourselves, than to load the memory with the thoughts of other men.--Beattie

Education does not mean teaching people to know what they do not know; it means teaching them to behave as they do not behave. --Ruskin

If a man empties his purse into his head, no man can take it away from him. An investment in knowledge always pays the best interest.--Franklin

Educate your children to self-control, to the habit of holding passion and prejudice and evil tendencies subject to an upright and reasoning will, and you have done much to abolish misery from their future lives and crimes from society.--Anon.

The problem of education is twofold: first to know, and then to utter. Everyone who lives any semblance of an inner life thinks more nobly and profoundly than he speaks.--R.L. Stevenson

Look out for the boy who has to plunge into work direct from the common school and who begins by sweeping out the office. He is probably the dark horse you had better watch.--Andrew Carnegie

He that has found a way to keep a child's spirit easy, active, and free, and yet at the same time to restrain him from many things he has a mind to, and to draw him to things that are uneasy to him, has, in my opinion, got the true secret of education.--Locke

Too much attention has been paid to making education attractive by smoothing the path as compared with inducing strenuous voluntary effort.--A.L. Lowell

The worst education that teaches self-denial is better than the best that teaches everything else and not that.--J. Sterling

Education is not learning; it is the exercise and development of the power of the mind; and the two great methods by which this end may be accomplished are in the halls of learning, or in the conflicts of life.--Princeton Review

If we work upon marble, it will perish; if on brass, time will efface it; if we rear temples, they will crumble into dust; but if we work upon immortal minds, and imbue them with principles, with the just fear of God and love of our fellow-men, we engrave on those tablets something that will brighten to all eternity.--Daniel Webster

ELOQUENCE

True eloquence consists in saying all that is proper, and nothing more.--Rochefoucauld

Brevity is a great charm of eloquence.--Cicero

Action is eloquence; the eyes of the ignorant are more learned than their ears.--Shakespeare

The clear conception, outrunning the deductions of logic, the high purpose, the firm resolve, the dauntless spirit, speaking on the tongue, beaming from the eye, informing every feature, and urging the whole man onward, right onward to his object.--this, this is eloquence; or rather it is something greater and higher than all eloquence; it is action, noble, sublime, godlike action.--Daniel Webster

It is of eloquence as of a flame; it requires matter to feed it, and motion to excite it; and it brightens as it burns.--Tacitus

Eloquence is in the assembly, not merely in the speaker.--William Pitt

Eloquence is the transference of thought and emotion from one heart to another, no matter how it is done.--John B. Gough

Eloquence is logic on fire.--Beecher

Eloquence is vehement simplicity.--Cecil

There is not less eloquence in the voice, the eye, the gesture, than in words.--Rochefoucauld

True eloquence does not consist in speech.--It cannot be brought from far.--Labor and learning may toil for it in vain.--Words and phrases may be marshalled in every way, but they cannot compass it.--It must consist in the man, in the subject, and in the occasion.--Webster

The pleasure of eloquence is, in greatest part, owing often to the stimulus of the occasion which produces it--to the magic of sympathy which exalts the feeling of each, by radiating on him the feeling of all.--Emerson

A word fitly spoken is like apples of gold in pictures of silver. --Solomon

Eloquence is the art of saying things in such a way that those to whom we speak may listen to them with pleasure.--Pascal

No man ever did or ever will become truly eloquent without being a constant reader of the Bible and an admirer of the purity and sublimity of its language.--Ames

He is an eloquent man who can treat humble subjects with delicacy, lofty things impressively, and moderate things temperately.--Cicero

ENCOURAGEMENT

Correction does much, but encouragement does more.--Encouragement after censure is as the sun after a shower.--Goethe

A smile of encouragement at the right moment may act like sunlight on a closed up flower, it may be the turning point for a struggling life.

A helping word to one in trouble is often like a switch on a railroad track--but one inch between a wreck and smooth rolling prosperity. --H.W. Beecher

I have never seen a man who could do real work except under the stimulus of encouragement and enthusiasm and the approval of the people of whom he is working.--Schwab

I believe that any man's life will be filled with constant and unexpected encouragement, if he makes up his mind to do his level best each day, and as nearly as possible reaching the highwater mark of pure and useful living.--B.T. Washington

We should seize every opportunity to give encouragement. Encouragement is oxygen to the soul. The days are always dark enough. There is no need for us to emphasize the fact by spreading further gloom.--George A. Adams

All may do what has by man been done.--Young

ENTHUSIASM

Every man is at his best when he adds enthusiasm to whatever he honestly believes in. Both power and progress will then enter into his undertakings.--John Wanamaker

Every great and commanding movement in the annals of the world is the triumph of enthusiasm.--Nothing great was ever achieved without it.--Emerson

Enthusiasm is a virtue rarely to be met with in seasons of calm and unruffled prosperity.--It flourishes in adversity, kindles in the hour of danger, and awakens to deeds of renown.--The terrors of persecution only serve to quicken the energy of its purposes.--It swells in proud integrity, and, great in the purity of its cause, it can scatter defiance amidst hosts of enemies.--Chalmers

The sense of this word among the Greeks affords the noblest definition of it; enthusiasm signifies "God in us."--Mad. De Stael

Every production of genius must be the production of enthusiasm. --Disraeli

Nothing is so contagious as enthusiasm.--It is the real allegory of the tale of Orpheus; it moves stones, and charms brutes.--It is the genius of sincerity, and truth accomplishes no victories without it.--Bulwer-Lytton

FAILURE

Any officer who is afraid of failure will never win! Any man who is afraid to die will never really live.--Gen. George Patton

To have failed once is not so much a pity as is to not try again. --Wanamaker

Men are born to succeed, not to fail.--Goethe

Failures are not fatal unless we go to sleep with them. Edison, Marconi, Cyrus, Field, Abraham Lincoln, Ulysses S. Grant had their failures, but each of them kept on undaunted until he "won out".

If I fail, it will be for lack of *ability*, and not of *purpose*.--Lincoln

Too many failures are traced to a lack of persistence and not lack of talent or ability.--Dr. Paul Parker

If you visualize a failure, you tend to create the conditions that produce failure. Visualize-believe-and thank God in advance.--N.V. Peale

Men do not fail; they give up trying.--Root

We can do worse than fail; we can succeed and be proud of our success and burn incense to our nets and despise those who fail and forget the Hand which both gives and withholds.--Fulton Sheen

FAITH

Faith affirms many things respecting which the senses are silent, but nothing which they deny.--It is superior to their testimony, but never opposed to it.--Pascal

Faith is like love: it cannot be forced.--As trying to force love begets hatred, so trying to compel religious belief leads to unbelief. --Schopenhauer

Despotism may govern without faith, but Liberty cannot.--De Tocqueville

Faith is to believe, on the word of God, what we do not see, and its reward is to see and enjoy what we believe.--Augustine

What I admire in Columbus is not his having discovered a world, but his having gone to search for it on the faith of an opinion.--Turgot

All I have seen teaches me to trust the Creator for all I have not seen. --Emerson

It is faith among men that holds the moral elements of society together, as it is faith in God that binds the world to his throne.--W.M. Evarts

The errors of faith are better than the best thoughts of unbelief. --Thomas Russell

Strike from mankind the principle of faith, and men would have no more history than a flock of sheep.--Bulwer-Lytton

FEAR

Fear kills more people than death.--Gen. George Patton

Fear is the tax that conscience pays to guilt.--Sewell

Present fears are less than horrible imaginings.--Shakespeare

God planted fear in the soul as truly as he planted hope or courage. --It is a kind of bell or gong which rings the mind into quick life and avoidance on the approach of danger.--It is the soul's signal for rallying.--H.W. Beecher

The remarkable thing about fearing God is that when you fear God you fear nothing else, whereas if you do not fear God you fear everything else. "Blessed is everyone that feareth the Lord."--Chambers

Fear is the mother of foresight.--H. Taylor

He who fears being conquered is sure of defeat.--Napoleon

Early and provident fear is the mother of safety.--Burke

It is only the fear of God that can deliver us from the fear of man. --Witherspoon

No one loves the man whom he fears.--Aristotle

FREEDOM

To have freedom is only to have that which is absolutely necessary to enable us to be what we ought to be, and to possess what we ought to possess.--Rahel

No man is free who is not master of himself.--Epictetus

The only freedom which deserves the name is that of pursuing our own good, in our own way, so long as we do not attempt to deprive others of theirs, or impede their efforts to obtain it.--J.S. Mill

He is the free man whom the truth makes free, and all are slaves beside.--Cowper

Freedom of religion, freedom of the press, and freedom of person under the protection of the habeas corpus, these are principles that have guided our steps through an age of revolution and reformation. --Jefferson

Men are free when they are in a living homeland. . .not when they are escaping to some wild west. The most unfree souls go west, and shout of freedom. Men are freest when they are most unconscious of freedom. The shout is the rattling of chains, always was.--D. H. Lawrence

Real freedom comes from the mastery, through knowledge, of historic conditions and race character which makes possible a free and intelligent use of experience for the purpose of progress.--H.W. Mabie

FRIENDSHIP

Friendships are fragile things, and require as much care in handling as any other fragile and precious thing.--R.S. Bourne

He alone has lost the art to live who cannot win new friends.--S. Weir Mitchell

Friendship improves happiness, and abates misery, by doubling our joy, and dividing our grief.--Addison

Those friends are weak and worthless, that will not use the privilege of friendship in admonishing their friends with freedom and confidence, as well of their errors as of their danger.--Bacon

The love of man to woman is a thing common and of course, and at first partakes more of instinct and passion than of choice; but true friendship between man and man is infinite and immortal.--Plato

We take care of our health, we lay up money, we make our roof tight and our clothing sufficient, but who provides wisely that he shall not be wanting in the best property of all--friends?--Emerson

Friendship is a plant of slow growth, and must undergo and withstand the shocks of adversity before it is entitled to the appellation. --Washington

Be slow to fall into friendship; but when thou art in, continue firm and constant.--Socrates

The difficulty is not so great to die for a friend, as to find a friend worth dying for.--Home

Friendship with God means that there is now something of the nature of God in a man on which God can base His friendship. --Oswald Chambers

The only way to have a friend is to be one.--Emerson

I desire to conduct the affairs of this administration so that if at the end, when I come to lay down the reins of power, I have lost every other friend on earth, I shall have at least one friend left, and that friend shall be down inside of me.--Lincoln

Much certainty of the happiness and purity of our lives depends on our making a wise choice of our companions and friends.--John Lubbock

A friend gives us confidence for life, a friend makes us outdo ourselves.--Lindsay

Be very careful in the selection of your friends: 'The most valuable
and fairest furniture of life.'--Cicero

Stretch a hand to one unfriended and thy loneliness is ended.
--Oxenham

GENEROSITY

A man there was and they called him mad; the more he gave the
more he had.--Bunyan

Just a little gift, costing one dollar, may give a thousand dollars'
worth of pleasure, and be a lifelong grateful memory.--John
Wanamaker

True generosity does not consist in obeying every impulse of humanity, in following blind passion for our guide, and impairing our circumstances by present benefactions, so as to render us incapable of
future ones.--Goldsmith

There is wisdom in generosity, as in everything else.--A friend to
everybody is often a friend to nobody; or else, in his simplicity, he
robs his family to help strangers, and so becomes brother to a beggar.
--Spurgeon

One great reason why men practice generosity so little in the world
is, their finding so little there: generosity is catching; and if so many
men escape it, it is in a great degree from the same reason that coun-
trymen escape the small-pox,--because they meet with no one to give
it them.--Greville

If there be any truer measure of a man than by what he does, it must
be by what he gives.--South

It is not enough to help the feeble up, but to support him after.
--Shakespeare

GRATITUDE

An attitude of gratitude flavors everything you do.--Paul Speicher

Gratitude takes three forms: a feeling in the heart, an expression in words, and a giving in return.--John Wanamaker

Gratitude to God makes even a temporal blessing a taste of heaven. --Romaine

He that urges gratitude pleads the cause both of God and men, for without it we can neither be sociable nor religious.--Seneca

To the generous mind the heaviest debt is that of gratitude, when it is not in our power to repay it.--Franklin

Gratitude is characteristic only of the humble. The egotistic are so impressed by their own importance that they take everything given them as if it were their due. They have no room in their hearts for recollection of the undeserved favors they received.--Fulton Sheen

He who acknowledges a kindness had it still, and he who has a grateful sense of it has requited it.--Cicero

O Lord, who lends me life, lend me a heart replete with thankfulness.--Shakespeare

God is pleased with no music below so much as with the thanksgiving songs of relieved widows and supported orphans; of rejoicing, comforted, and thankful persons.--Jeremy Taylor

GREATNESS

A great man is not tied to his own opinions, his hates, his preferences, or his prejudices, but is big enough to weigh existing circumstances and passing events.--John Wanamaker

A really great man is known by three signs--generosity in the design, humanity in the execution, moderation in success.--Bismarck

If any man seeks for greatness, let him forget greatness and ask for truth, and he will find both.--Horace Mann

61

He only is great who has the habits of greatness; who, after performing what none in ten thousand could accomplish, passes on like Samson, and "tells neither father nor mother of it."--Lavater

The price of greatness is responsibility.--Churchill

There never was any heart truly great and gracious, that was not also tender and compassionate.--South

Not a day passes over the earth but men and women of no note do great deeds, speak great words, and suffer noble sorrows. Of these obscure heroes, philosophers, and martyrs the greater part will never be known till that hour when many that were great shall be small, and the small great.--Charles Reade

Great men are the commissioned guides of mankind, who rule their fellows because they are wiser.--Carlyle

Everything great is not always good, but all good things are great. --Demosthenes

No man has come to true greatness who has not felt in some degree that his life belongs to his race, and that what God gives him he gives him for mankind.--Phillips Brooks

It is easy in the world to live after the world's opinion--it is easy in solitude to live after your own; but the great man is he who, in the midst of the world, keeps with perfect sweetness the independence of solitude.--Emerson

If the title of great man ought to be reserved for him who cannot be charged with an indiscretion or a vice; who spent his life in establishing the independence, the glory, and durable prosperity of his country; who succeeded in all that he undertook, and whose successes were never won at the expense of honor, justice, integrity, or by the sacrifice of a single principle--this title will not be denied to Washington.--Sparks

Some are born great; some achieve greatness; and some have greatness thrust upon them.--Shakespeare

A great man is one who affects the mind of his generation.--Disraeli

There never was yet a truly great man that was not at the same time truly virtuous.--Franklin

When Nature removes a great man, people explore the horizon for a successor; but none comes, and none will.--Emerson

GROWTH

It is best for a man to grow where he is planted.--John Wanamaker

Every oak was once an acorn.--Wheeler

Everybody wants to be somebody; nobody wants to grow.--Goethe

The purpose of learning is growth, and our minds, unlike our bodies, can continue growing as we continue to live.--Adler

Life consists of melting illusions, correcting mistakes and replacing outgrown clothing. But, I remind myself, there is no other way to grow.--A.P. Gouthey

90% of all growth is spiritual.--Mooreland Wright

An acorn is not an oak tree when it is sprouted. It must go through long summers and fierce winters; it has to endure all that frost and snow and side-striking winds can bring before it is a full grown oak. These are rough teachers; but rugged schoolmasters make rugged pupils. So a man is not a man when he is created; he is only begun. His manhood must come with years.--H.W. Beecher

Nothing is lost upon a man who is bent upon growth; nothing is wasted on one who is always preparing for his work and his life by keeping eyes, mind, and heart open to nature, men, books, experience. Such a man finds ministers to his education on all sides; everything cooperates with his passion for growth.--H. Mabie

The purpose of life is spiritual, mental, and physical growth.--Blandi

HABIT

The great advantage of habit is that it saves us a lot of attention, effort and brain work.--Fulton Sheen

Habit is a cable.--We weave a thread of it every day, and at last we cannot break it.--H. Mann

Habit is the deepest law of human nature.--Carlyle

When we have practiced good actions awhile, they become easy; when they are easy, we take pleasure in them; when they please us, we do them frequently; and then, by frequency of act, they grow into a habit.--Tillotson

Habit is either the best of servants, or the worst of masters.--Emmons

Habit, if not resisted, soon becomes necessity.--Augustine

The chains of habit are generally too small to be felt until they are too strong to be broken.--Johnson

The phrases that men hear or repeat continually, end by becoming convictions and ossify the organs of intelligence.--Goethe

Habit, to which all of us are more or less slaves.--Fontaine

We have to work out what God works in, and the way we work it out is by the mechanical process of habit.--Chambers

The underlying cause of all weakness and unhappiness in man has always been, and still is, weak habit-of-thought.--Horace Fletcher

There are habits, not only of drinking, swearing, and lying, but of every modification of action, speech, and thought. Man is a bundle of habits; in a word, there is not a quality or function, either of body or mind, which does not feel the influence of this great law of animated nature.--Paley

What a curious phenomenon it is that you can get men to die for the liberty of the world who will not make the little sacrifice that is needed to free themselves from their own individual bondage.--Bruce Barton

Habits work more constantly and with greater force than reason, which, when we have most need of it, is seldom fairly consulted, and more rarely obeyed.--Locke

Habit, if wisely and skillfully formed, becomes truly a second nature; but unskillfully and unmethodically directed, it will be as it were the ape of nature, which imitates nothing to the life, but only clumsily and awkwardly.--Bacon

Most of the difficulty in forming a special habit is that we will not discipline ourselves.--Oswald Chambers

HAPPINESS

Be happy with what you have, and better things will come along. --John Wanamaker

The more we give happiness, the more we have left.--John Wanamaker

The world would be both better and brighter if we would dwell on the duty of happiness, as well as on the happiness of duty.--Sir J. Lubbock

No man is happy who does not think himself so.--Marcus Antoninus

Happiness is neither within us only, or without us; it is the union of ourselves with God.--Pascal

Happiness consists in being perfectly satisfied with what we have got and with what we haven't got.--Anon.

It is not how much we have, but now much we enjoy, that makes happiness.--Spurgeon

I am more and more convinced that our happiness or unhappiness depends far more on the way we meet the events of life, than on the nature of those events themselves.--Humboldt

Seek happiness for its own sake, and you will not find it; seek for duty, and happiness will follow as the shadow comes with the sunshine.--Tryon Edwards

Happiness is dependent on the taste, and not on things.--It is by having what we like that we are made happy, not by having what others think desirable.--Rouchefoucauld

Men of the noblest dispositions think themselves happiest when others share their happiness with them.--Jeremy Taylor

All who would win joy, must share it; happiness was born a twin.
--Byron

Happiness consists in the attainment of our desires, and in our having only right desires.--Augustine

The strength and the happiness of a man consists in finding out the way in which God is going, and going in that way, too.--H.W. Beecher

Call no man happy till you know the end of his life. Till then, at most, he can only be counted fortunate.--Herodotus

The belief that youth is the happiest time of life is founded on a fallacy. The happiest person is the person who thinks the most interesting thoughts, and we grow happier as we grow older.--William Lyon Phelps

The secret of happiness is renunciation.--Andrew Carnegie

I see in this world two heaps--one of happiness, and the other of misery. Now, if I can take but the smallest bit from the second, and add it to the first, I carry a point. I should be glad indeed to do great things; but I will not neglect such little ones as this.--John Newton

The habit of being happy enables one to be freed, or largely freed, from the domination of outward conditions.--Robert Louis Stevenson

Do not speak of your happiness to one less fortunate than yourself.
--Plutarch

True happiness renders men kind and sensible; and that happiness is always shared with others.--Montesquieu

There is but one way to tranquility of mind and happiness; let this, therefore, be always ready at hand with thee, both when thou wakest early in the morning, and all the day long, and when thou goest late to sleep, to account no external things thine own, but commit all these to God.--Epictetus

The most happy man is he who knows how to bring into relation the end and the beginning of his life.--Goethe

The great high-road of human welfare and happiness lies along the highway of steadfast well-doing, and they who are the most persistent and work in the truest spirit, will invariably be the most successful.--S. Smiles

To be happy you must forget yourself.--Learn benevolence; it is the only cure of a morbid temper.--Bulwer-Lytton

HEAVEN

The love of heaven makes one heavenly.--Shakespeare

If I ever reach heaven I expect to find three wonders there: first, to meet some I had not thought to see there; second, to miss some I had expected to see there; and third, the greatest wonder of all, to find myself there.--John Newton

Every saint in heaven is as a flower in the garden of God, and holy love is the fragrance and sweet odor that they all sent forth, and with which they fill the bowers of that paradise above. Every soul there is as a note in some concert of delightful music, that sweetly harmonizes with every other note, and all together blend in the most rapturous strains in praising God and the Lamb forever.--J. Edwards

Heaven must be in me before I can be in heaven.--Stanford

It is heaven only that is given away--only God may be had for the asking.--J.R. Lowell

I would not give one moment of heaven for all the joy and riches of the world, even if it lasted for thousands and thousands of years.
--Luther

Who seeks for heaven alone to save his soul may keep the path, but will not reach the goal; while he who walks in love may wander far, yet God will bring him where the blessed are.--Henry Van Dyke

Nothing is farther than the earth from heaven; nothing is nearer than heaven to earth.--Hare

Heaven, the treasury of everlasting joy.--Shakespeare

If the way to heaven be narrow, it is not long; and if the gate be straight, it opens into endless life.--Beveridge

Think of heaven with hearty purpose and premptory designs to get thither.--Taylor

The hope of heaven under troubles is like wind and sails to the soul. --Rutherford

Earth has no sorrow that heaven cannot heal.--Moore

Above all. Heaven is above all yet; there sits a judge that no king shall corrupt.--Shakespere

The city which God has prepared is as imperishable in its inhabitants as its materials. Its pearl, its jasper, its pure gold, are only immortal to frame the abode of immortals. No cry of death is in any of its dwellings. No funeral darkens along any of its way. No sepulcher of the holiest relics gleams among the everlasting hills. "Violence is not heard in the land." "There is no more death." Its very name has per-ished. "Is swallowed up in victory."--R.W. Hamilton

HELL

Hell is the place of angelic condemnation. It has nothing to do pri-marily with man. God's Book never says that hell was made for man, although it is true that it is the only place for the man who rejects God's salvation. Hell was the result of a distinct condemnation passed by God on celestial beings, and is as eternal as those celestial anarchists.--Oswald Chambers

Hell is but the collected ruins of the moral world, and sin is the prin-ciple that has made them.--Anon.

Hell is truth seen too late--Duty neglected in its season.--Tryon Edwards

When the world dissolves, all places will be hell that are not heaven. --Marlow

If there is any subject which is offensive to modern sentimentalists it is the subject of hell. Our generation clamors for what the poet has called "a soft dean, who never mentions hell to ears polite", and our unsouled age wants a Christianity watered so as to make the Gospel of Christ nothing more than a gentle doctrine of good will, a social program of economic betterment, and a mild scheme of progressive idealism.--Sheen

Hell is the full knowledge of the truth, when truth, resisted long, is sworn our foe, and calls eternity to do her right.--Young

HEROISM

Fear nothing so much as sin, and your moral heroism is complete. --C. Simmons

The grandest of heroic deeds are those which are performed within four walls and in domestic privacy.--Richter

The man who rules his spirit, saith the voice that cannot err, is greater than the one who takes a city.--If each would have dominion of himself, would govern wisely, and thus show true courage, knowledge, power, benevolence, all the princely soul of private virtues, then each would be a prince--a hero--a man in likeness of his maker.--Mrs. S.J. Hale

Every man is a hero and an oracle to somebody, and to that person, whatever he says, has an enhanced value.--Emerson

The world's battlefields have been in the heart chiefly; more heroism has been displayed in the household and the closet, than on the most memorable battlefields of history.--H.W.Beecher

The greatest obstacle to being heroic is the doubt whether one may not be going to prove one's self a fool.--The truest heroism is to resist the doubt; and the profoundest wisdom to know when it ought to be resisted and when obeyed.--Hawthorne

Unbounded courage and compassion joined proclaim him good and great, and make the hero and the man complete.--Addison

The heroes of mankind are the mountain, the highlands of the moral world.--A.P. Stanley

HISTORY

History is His story.--Abram Veradie

History is little more than the register of the crimes, follies, and misfortunes of mankind.--Gibbon

History is a voice forever sounding across the centuries the laws of right and wrong. Opinions alter, manners change, creeds rise and fall, but the moral law is written on the tablets of eternity.--Froude

We read history through our prejudices.--Wendell Phillips

The men who make history, have not time to write it.--Metternich
God is in the facts of history as truly as he is in the march of the seasons, the revolutions of the planets, or the architecture of the worlds.
--J. Lanahan

This I hold to be the chief office of history, to rescue virtuous actions from the oblivion to which a want of records would consign them, and that men should feel a dread of being considered infamous in the opinions of posterity, from their depraved expressions and base actions.--Tacitus

The best thing which we derive from history is the enthusiasm that it raises in us.--Goethe

Grecian history is a poem; Latin history, a picture; modern history a chronicle.--Chateaubriand

All history is but a romance, unless it is studied as an example. --Croly

Biography is the only true history.--Carlyle

History is the first distinct product of man's spiritual nature, his earliest expression of what can be called thought.--Carlyle

Those who do not know history are forever condemned to repeat it. --Durant

Not to know what has been transacted in former times is to be always a child.--If no use is made of the labors of past ages, the world must remain always in the infancy of knowledge.--Cicero

Those who have employed the study of history, as they ought, for their instruction, for the regulation of their private manner, and the management of public affairs, must agree with me that it is the most pleasant school of wisdom.--Dryden

Jesus Christ did not evolve out of history, He came into history from outside history; He is not the best human being the world has ever seen, He is a Being who cannot be accounted for by the human race at all.--Oswald Chambers

Fellow-citizens, we cannot escape history. We. . .will be remembered in spite of ourselves. No personal significance of insignificance can spare one or another of us. The fiery trial through which we pass will light us down in honor or dishonor, to the latest generation.--Lincoln

HOPE

The miserable hath no other medicine but only hope.--Shakespeare

Hope is the most beneficial of all the affections, and doth much to the prolongation of life, if it be not too often frustrated, but entertaineth the fancy with an expectation of good.--Bacon

In all things it is better to hope than to despair.--Goethe

Hope is brightest when it dawns from fears.--Walter Scott

Hope is the best possession.--None are completely wretched but those who are without hope, and few are reduced so low as that. --Hazlitt

Hope writes the poetry of the boy, but memory that of the man. Man looks forward with smiles, but backward with sighs. Such is the wise providence of God. The cup of life is sweetness at the brim--the flavor is impaired as we drink deeper, and the dregs are made bitter that we may not struggle when it is taken from our lips.--Emerson

Before you give up hope, turn back and read the attacks that were made upon Lincoln.--Bruce Barton

HUMILITY

Don't be so humble, you're not that good.--Golda Meir

There is nothing more awful than conscious humility, it is the most Satanic type of pride.--Oswald Chambers

True humility is not an abject, groveling, self-despising spirit, it is but a right estimate of ourselves as God sees us.--Tryon Edwards

Sense shines with a double luster when it is set in humility. An able and yet humble man is a jewel worth a kingdom.--Penn

I believe the first test of a truly great man is his humility.--Ruskin

The doctrines of grace humble man without degrading, and exalt without inflating him.--Charles Hodge

It was pride that changed angels into devils; it is humility that makes men as angels.--Augustine

They that know God will be humble; they that know themselves cannot be proud.--Flavel

Humility is the genuine proof of Christian virtue.--Without it we keep all our defects; and they are only crusted over by pride, which conceals them from others, and often from ourselves. --Rouchfoucauld

Humility is to have a right estimate of one's self--not to think less of himself than he ought.--The higher a man is in grace, the lower will he be in his own esteem.--Spurgeon

There is nothing so clear-sighted and sensible as a noble mind in a low estate.--Jane Porter

Should you ask me, 'What is the first thing in religion?' I should reply, the first, second, and third thing therein--nay, all--is humility. --Augustine

God walks with the humble; he reveals himself to the lowly; he gives understanding to the little ones; he discloses his meaning to pure minds, but hides his grace from the curious and the proud.--Thomas. A. Kempis

Humility in relation to love means thinking others better than ourselves. One advantage of this is that it gives us some examples to imitate. Pride, on the other hand, sometimes seeks first place that others may say, "Oh! What greatness!" Pride, too, can subtly take the *last* place that others may say, "What humility!"--Fulton Sheen

It is in vain to gather virtues without humility; for the spirit of God delights to dwell in the hearts of the humble.--Erasmus

Humility is not an ideal, it is the unconscious result of the life being rightly related to God.--Oswald Chambers.

After crosses and losses men grow humbler and wiser.--Franklin

HUMOR

Wit may be a thing of pure imagination, but humor involves sentiment and character.--Humor is of a genial quality; dwells in the same character with pathos, and it always mingled with sensibility.--Giles

I live in a constant endeavor to fence against the infirmities of ill-health, and other evils of life, by mirth. I am persuaded that every time a man smiles--but much more so when he laughs--it adds something to this fragment of life.--Sterne

There is certainly no defense against adverse fortune which is, on the whole, so effectual as an habitual sense of humor.--T.W. Higginson

True humor springs not more from the head than from the heart.--It is not contempt; its essence is love.--It issues not in laughter, but in still smiles, which lie far deeper.--Carlyle

Good humor is one of the best articles of dress one can wear in society.--Thackeray

With the fearful strain that is on me night and day, if I did not laugh I should die.--Abraham Lincoln

For health and the constant enjoyment of life, give me a keen and ever present sense of humor; it is the next best thing to an abiding faith in providence.--G.B. Cheever

IDEALS & IDEAS

Ideas and ideals really become the foundation of the main track of life.--John Wanamaker

The best and noblest lives are those which are set toward high ideals. And the highest and noblest ideal that any man can have is Jesus of Nazareth.--Almeron

Ideals are the world's masters.--J.G. Holland

Great objects form great minds.--Emmons

We never reach our ideals, whether of mental or moral improvement, but the thought of them shows us our deficiencies, and spurs us on to higher and better things.--Tryon Edwards

What we need most, is not so much to realize the ideal as to idealize the real.--Hedge

Many ideas grow better when transplanted into another mind than in the one where they sprung up. That which was a weed in one becomes a flower in the other, and a flower again dwindles down to a mere weed by the same change. Healthy growths may become poisonous by falling upon the wrong mental soil, and what seemed a night-shade in one mind unfolds as a morning-glory in the other. --O.W. Holmes

Ideas control the world.--Garfield

An idea, like a ghost, according to the common notion of ghosts, must be spoken to a little before it will explain itself.--Dickens

Temples have their images; and we see what influence they have always had over a great part of mankind.--But, in truth, the ideas and images in men's minds are the invisible powers that constantly govern them; and to these they all pay universally a ready submission. --J. Edwards

74

It is not possible for any man to have all the good ideas.--John Wanamaker

Matter--the most important thing in the world? No! Ideals! Companionship of inspiring heroes, martyrs, saints, teachers, leaders. These are the indispensables for human achievement. Man cannot live without the support of other human personalities--wise, friendly, and compassionate.--Liebman

By what strange law of mind is it, that an idea long overlooked, and trodden under foot as a useless stone, suddenly sparkles out in new light as a discovered diamond?--Mrs. Stowe

Ideas go booming through the world louder than cannon. Thoughts are mightier than armies. Principles have achieved more victories than horsemen or chariots.--W.M. Paxton

Ideas are cosmopolitan.--They have the liberty of the world.--You have no right to take the sword and cross the bounds of other nations, and enforce on them laws or institutions they are unwilling to receive.--But there is no limit to the sphere of ideas. Your thoughts and feelings, the whole world lies open to them, and you have the right to send them into any latitude, and to give them sweep around the earth, to the mind of every human being.--H.W. Beecher

A man's ideals in life are his measuring rod of success in life. But they do not automatically give him success. For that effort is necessary. Nor is the exertion of effort, alone, enough; a great deal depends upon how this is done. Success in life must be recognized as a double problem--of ideals in life, and the means used to realize them.--Councillor

He who wishes to fulfill his mission in the world must be a man of one idea, that is of one great overmastering purpose, overshadowing all his aims, and guiding and controlling his entire life.--Bate

When young men are beginning life, the most important period, it is often said, is that in which their habits are formed.--That is a very important period.--But the period in which the ideas of the young are formed and adopted is more important still.--For the ideal with which you go forth to measure things determines the nature, so far as you are concerned, of everything you meet.--H.W. Beecher

75

If one can put it reverently, unless God Almighty can become concrete and actual, He is nothing to me but a mental abstraction, because an ideal has no power unless it can be realized.--Chambers

IMAGINATION

We are all of us imaginative in some form or other, for images are the brood of desire.--George Eliot

Many have no happier moments than those that they pass in solitude, abandoned to their won imagination, which sometimes puts scepters in their hands or miters on their heads, shifts the scene of pleasure with endless variety, bids all the forms of beauty sparkle before them, and gluts them with every change of visionary luxury. --Johnson

A vile imagination, once indulged, gets the key of our minds, and can get in again very easily, whether we will or no, and can so return as to bring seven other spirits with it more wicked than itself; and what may follow no one knows.--Spurgeon

He who has imagination without learning has wings and no feet. --Joubert

Imagination rules the world.--Napoleon

Imagination is the eye of the soul.--Joubert

The soul without imagination is what an observatory would be without a telescope.--H.W. Beecher

Imagination disposes of everything; it creates beauty, justice, and happiness, which are everything in this world.--Pascal

Imagination is the eye of the soul.--Joubert

INFLUENCE

The people who influence us are those who have stood unconsciously for the right thing, they are like the stars and the lilies, and the joy of God flows through them all the time.--Oswald Chambers

An educated man just teaches the thing that he has been taught, and it's the same that everyone else has been taught that has read and studied the same books that he has.--Will Rogers

I am a part of all that I have met.--Tennyson

The humblest individual exerts some influence, either for good or evil, upon others.--Beecher

No human being can come into this world without increasing or diminishing the sum total of human happiness.--Elihu Burritt

If I can put one touch of a rosy sunset into the life of any man or woman, I shall feel that I have worked with God.--George MacDonald

There is no end to the influence of women on our life. It is at the bottom of everything that happens to us.--Disraeli

The whole earth is the tomb of heroic men, and their story is not graven only on stone over their clay, but abides everywhere, without a visible symbol, woven into the stuff of other men's lives. --Thucydides

INTEGRITY

Our integrity is never worth so much as when we have parted with our all to keep it.--Colton

Give us a man, young or old, high or low, on whom we know we can thoroughly depend--who will stand firm when others fail--the friend faithful and true, the adviser honest and fearless, the adversary just and chivalrous; in such a one there is a fragment of the Rock of Ages --a sign that there has been a prophet amongst us.--Dean Stanley

Though a hundred crooked paths may conduct to a temporary success, the one plain and straight path of public and private virtue can alone lead to a pure and lasting fame and the blessings of posterity. --Edward Everett

Integrity without knowledge is weak and useless.--Johnson

Both wit and understanding are trifles without integrity. The ignorant peasant without fault is greater than the philosopher with many. What is genius or courage without a heart?--Goldsmith

Aaron Burr was a more brilliant man than George Washington. If he had been loyal to truth, he would have been an abler man; but that which made George Washington the chief hero in our great republic was the sagacity, not of intellectual genius, but of the moral element in him.--A.E. Dunning

JUDGMENT

Have you ever noticed that the straightest stick is crooked in the water? In forming judgments of others, or in passing opinions upon current topics, let us go slow and be careful until we know all the existing circumstances.--John Wanamaker

The morning after excessive drinking, the head with its hangover makes a judgment on intemperance, as during the night the sick stomach passes judgment on the food that was not good for digestion. As audiences make judgment on a play by their applause, so there is to be a final accountability for the thoughts and the words and deeds of every human heart. In vain is it to be expected that we who pass judgment constantly on others should not pass in judgment ourselves.--Fulton Sheen

Forbear to judge, for we are sinners all.--Shakespeare

Some people, without knowing it, carry with them a magnifying glass, with which they see, when they wish, other people's imperfections.--John Wanamaker

Extreme justice is extreme injustice.--Cicero

In every life there is one place where God must have 'elbow room'. We must not pass judgment on others, nor must we make a principle of judging out of our own experience. It is impossible for a man to know the views of Almighty God.--Chambers

KINDNESS

I expect to pass through life but once. If therefore, there be any kindness I can show, or any good thing I can do to any fellow being, let me do it now, and not defer or neglect it, as I shall not pass this way again.--William Penn

Kindness is the golden chain by which society is bound together. --Goethe

The drying up a single tear, has more of honest fame, than shedding seas of gore.--Byron

Kindness in women, not their beauteous looks, shall win my love. --Shakespeare

Kind looks, kind words, kind acts, and warm handshakes--these are secondary means of grace when men are in trouble and are fighting their unseen battles.--John Hall

The best portion of a good man's life is his little, nameless, unremembered acts of kindness and of love.--Wordsworth

A kind heart is a fountain of gladness, making everything in its vicinity freshen into smiles.--Washington Irving

It is good for us to think no grace or blessing truly ours till we are aware that God has blessed some one else with it through us. --Phillips Brooks

The happiness of life may be greatly increased by small courtesies in which there is no parade, whose voice is too still to tease, and which manifest themselves by tender and affectionate looks, and little kind acts of attention.--Sterne

Kind words produce their own image in men's souls; and a beautiful image it is. They soothe and quiet and comfort the hearer. They shame him out of his sour, morose, unkind feelings. We have not yet begun to use kind words in such abundance as they ought to be used.--Pascal

Ask thyself, daily, to how many ill-minded persons thou hast shown a kind disposition.--Marcus Antoninus

I had rather never receive a kindness, than never bestow one.--Not to return a benefit is the greater sin, but not to confer it, is the earlier. --Seneca

I wonder why it is that we are not all kinder to each other than we are. How much the world needs it! How easily it is done.--Henry Drummond

What do we live for, if it is not to make life less difficult to each other?--George Eliot

The cheapest of all things is kindness, its exercise requiring the least possible trouble and self-sacrifice.--Smiles

Make a rule, and pray to God to help you to keep it, never, if possible, to lie down at night without being able to say: "I have made one human being at least a little wiser, or a little happier, or at least a little better this day."--C. Kingsley

Let us open up our natures, throw wide the doors of our hearts and let in the sunshine of good will and kindness.--Marden

KNOWLEDGE

Knowledge and experience are the best two feet any one can have to equip him for successful living.--John Wanamaker

The first step to knowledge is to know that we are ignorant.--Cecil

We know accurately only when we know little; with knowledge doubt increases.--Goethe

The expression, "Knowledge is power," is used by Lord Bacon; but it had its origin long before his time, in the saying of Solomon, that "a wise man is strong: yea, a man of knowledge increaseth strength." Socrates said that a knowledge of our own ignorance is the first step toward true knowledge.--And Coleridge said, "We cannot make another comprehend our knowledge until we first comprehend his ingnorance."--Anon.

"Knowledge," says Bacon, "is power"; but mere knowledge is not power; it is only possibility. Action is power; and its highest manifestation is when it is directed by knowledge.--T.W. Palmer

Whatever our intellectual calling, no kind of knowledge is antagonistic to it.--All varieties of knowledge blend with, harmonize, and enrich the one kind of knowledge to which we attach our reputation. --Bulwer-Lytton

The love of knowledge in a young mind is almost a warrant against the infirm excitement of passions and vices.--H.W. Beecher

Knowledge and timber should not be much used until they are seasoned.--O.W. Holmes

Nothing in this life, after health and virtue, is more estimable than knowledge,--nor is there anything so easily attained, or so cheaply purchased,--the labor, only sitting still, and the expense but time, which, if we do not spend, we cannot save.--Sterne

The more extensive a man's knowledge of what has been done, the greater will be his power of knowing what to do.--Disraeli

Knowledge of our duties is the most essential part of the philosophy of life. If you escape duty you avoid action. The world demands results.--George W. Goethals

Knowledge is a comfortable and necessary retreat and shelter for us in advanced age, and if we do not plant it while young, it will give us no shade when we grow old.--Chesterfield

All wish to possess knowledge, but few, comparatively speaking, are willing to pay the price.--Juvenal

If a man empties his purse into his head, no one can take it away from him.--An investment in knowledge always pays the best interest. --Franklin

The best part of our knowledge is that which teaches us where knowledge leaves off and ignorance begins.--O.W. Holmes

LAUGHTER

It is a good thing to laugh, at any rate, and if a straw can tickle a man, it is an instrument of happiness. Beasts can weep when they suffer, but they cannot laugh.--Dryden

Even this vein of laughing, as I could produce out of grave authors, hath oftentimes a strong and sinewy force in teaching and comforting.--Milton

Beware of him who hates the laugh of a child.--Lavater

Man is the only creature endowed with the power of laughter; is he not also the only one that deserves to be laughed at?--Greville

Life without laughing is a dreary blank.--Thackeray

Laughter is a most healthful exertion; it is one of the greatest helps to digestion with which I am acquainted; and the custom prevalent among our fore-fathers, of exciting it at table by jesters and buffoons, was founded on true medical principles.--Hufeland

I like the laughter that opens the lips and the heart, that shows at the same time pearls and the soul.--Victor Hugo

One good, hearty laugh is a bombshell exploding in the right place, while spleen and discontent are a gun that kicks over the man who shoots it off.--Talmage

Conversation never sits easier than when we now and then discharge ourselves in a symphony of laughter; which may not improperly be called the chorus of conversation.--Steele

Next to a good soul-stirring prayer is a good laugh, when it is promoted by what is pure in itself and in its grotesque application.--Mutchmore

I am persuaded that every time a man smiles, but much more when he laughs, it adds something to this fragment of life.--Sterne

That laughter costs too much which is purchased by the sacrifice of decency.--Quintilian

Men show their character in nothing more clearly than by what they think laughable.--Goethe

A laugh, to be joyous, must flow from a joyous heart, for without kindness there can be no true joy.--Carlyle

The man who cannot laugh is not only fit for treasons, stratagems, and spoils; but his whole life is already a treason and a stratagem. --Carlyle

Laugh if you are wise.--Martial

And still, laughter is akin to weeping.--Lavater

Give me an honest laughter.--Scott

Then let us laugh. It is the cheapest luxury man enjoys, and, as Charles Lamb says, "is worth a hundred groans in any state of the market." It stirs up the blood, expands the chest, electrifies the nerves, clears away the cobwebs from the brain, and gives the whole system a shock to which the voltaic pile is as nothing. Nay, its delicious alchemy converts even tears into the quintessence of merriment, and makes wrinkles themselves expressive of youth and frolic.--W. Matthews

God made both tears and laughter, and both for kind purposes; for as laughter enables mirth and surprise to breathe freely, so tears enable sorrow to vent itself patiently. Tears hinder sorrow from becoming despair and madness.--Leigh Hunt

Laugh and the world laughs with you.--Ella Wheeler Wilcox

People who do not know how to laugh, are always pompous and self-conceited.--Thackeray

Laughter and weeping are the two intensest forms of human emotion, and these profound wells of human emotion are to be consecrated to God.--Oswald Chambers

LEARNING

Learning is better worth than house or land.--Crabbe

No man can ever lack this mortification of his vanity, that what he knows is but a very little in comparison of what he is ignorant of. Consider this, and instead of boasting thy knowledge of a few things, confess and be out of countenance for the many more which thou dost not understand.--Thomas a Kempis

The learning and knowledge that we have, is, at the most, but little compared with that of which we are ignorant.--Plato

Learning teaches how to carry things in suspense, without prejudice, till you resolve.--Bacon

The sweetest and most inoffensive path of life leads through the avenues of science and learning; and whoever can either remove any obstruction in this way, or open up any new prospect, ought, so far, to be esteemed a benefactor to mankind.--Hume

It is easy to learn something about everything, but difficult to learn everything about anything.--Emmons

He that wants good sense is unhappy in having learning, for he has thereby only more ways of exposing himself; and he that has sense, knows that learning is not knowledge, but rather the art of using it.
--Steele

The great art of learning, is to undertake but little at a time.--Locke

Seeing much, suffering much, and studying much, are the three pillars of learning.--Disraeli

Till a man can judge whether they be truths or no, his understanding is but little improved, and thus men of much reading, though greatly learned, but may be little knowing.--Locke

Learning gives us a fuller conviction of the imperfections of our nature; which one would think, might dispose us to modesty: for the more a man knows, the more he discovers his ignorance.--Jeremy Collier

Learning makes a man fit company for himself.--Young

It adds a precious seeing to the eye.--Shakespeare

O this learning, what a thing it is!--Shakespeare

Learning hath gained most by those books by which the printers have lost.--Thomas Fuller

Learning, to be of much use, must have a tendency to spread itself among the common people.--Henry Ward Beecher

If you want learning, you must work for it.--J.G. Holland

We should ask not who is the most learned, but who is the best learned.--Montaigne

Learning passes for wisdom among those who want both.--Sir W. Temple

Wear your learning like your watch, in a private pocket; and do not pull it out and strike it, merely to show that you have one. --Chesterfield

He who learns and makes no use of his learning, is a beast of burden, with a load of books. Comprehendeth the ass whether he carries on his back a library or a bundle of fagots?--Saadi

Men learn while they teach.--Seneca

Learning maketh young men temperate, is the comfort of old age, standing for wealth with poverty, and serving as an ornament to riches.--Cicero

Many persons, after they become learned cease to be good; all other knowledge is hurtful to him who has not the science of honesty and good nature.--Montaigne

The end of learning is to know God, and out of that knowledge to love Him, and to imitate Him, as we may the nearest, by possessing our souls of true virtue.--Milton

LIBERTY

The greatest glory of a free-born people, is to transmit that freedom to their children.--Havard

True liberty consists only in the power of doing what we ought to will, and in not being constrained to do what we ought not to will. --Johnathan Edwards

We hold these truths to be self-evident, that all men are created equal; that they are endowed by their Creator with inalienable rights; and that among these are life, liberty, and the pursuit of happiness. --Jefferson

Is life so dear, or peace so sweet as to be purchased at the price of chains and slavery?--Forbid it, Almighty God!--I know not what course others may take, but, as for me, give me liberty or give me death.--Patrick Henry

Liberty is not the right of one, but of all.--Herbert Spencer

Liberty, without wisdom, is license.--Burke

The liberty of a people consists in being governed by laws which they have made themselves, under whatsoever form it be of government; the liberty of a private man is being master of his own time and actions, as far as may consist with the laws of God, and of his country.--Cowley

If the true spark of religious and civil liberty be kindled, it will burn. Human agency cannot extinguish it. Like the earth's central fire, it may be smothered for a time; the ocean may overwhelm it; mountains may press it down; but its inherent and unconquerable force will heave both the ocean and the land, and at some time or another, in some place or another, the volcano will break out and flame to heaven.--Daniel Webster

Interwoven is the love of liberty with every ligament of the heart. --Washington

There is no liberty to men whose passions are stronger than their religious feelings; there is no liberty to men in whom ignorance predominates over knowledge; there is no liberty to men who know not how to govern themselves.--H.W. Beecher

Liberty is quite as much a moral as a political growth,--the result of free individual action, energy, and independence.--Smiles

Do you wish to be free? Then above all things, love God, love your neighbor, love one another, love the common weal; then you will have true liberty.--Savonarola

Reason and virtue alone can bestow liberty.--Shaftesbury

Eternal vigilance is the price of liberty.--John Philpot Curran

There are two freedoms--the false, where a man is free to do what he likes; the true, where a man is free to do what he ought.--Charles Kingsley

Liberty is worth whatever the best civilization is worth.--Henry Giles

The God who gave us life gave us liberty at the same time.--Jefferson

God grants liberty only to those who love it, and are always ready to guard and defend it.--Daniel Webster

Liberty, when it begins to take root, is a plant of rapid growth.--G. Washington

The love of liberty with life is given.--Dryden

Where slavery is, there liberty cannot be; and where liberty is, there slavery cannot be.--Abraham Lincoln

Liberty is to the collective body what health is to every individual body. Without health no pleasure can be tasted by man; without liberty, no happiness can be enjoyed by society.--Bolingbroke

Liberty **** is one of the choicest gifts that heaven hath bestowed upon man, and exceeds in value all the treasures which the earth contains within its bosom, or the sea covers.--Liberty, as well as honor, man ought to preserve at the hazard of his life, for without it life is insupportable.--Cervantes

Liberty must be limited in order to be enjoyed.--Burke

Liberty is a slow fruit.--Emerson

LIBRARIES

Next to acquiring good friends, the best acquisition is that of good books.--Colton

The student has his Rome, his Florence, his whole glowing Italy, within the four walls of his library. He has in his books the ruins of an antique world and the glories of a modern one.--Longfellow

What laborious days, what watchings by the midnight lamp, what rackings of the brain, what hopes and fears, what long lives of laborious study, are here sublimized into print, and condensed into the narrow compass of these surrounding shelves!--Horace Smith

My books are my tools, and the greater their variety and perfection the greater the help to my literary work.--Tryon Edwards.

Libraries are as the shrines where all the relics of saints, full of true virtue, and that without delusion or imposture, are preserved and reposed.--Bacon

A library is a land of shadows.--H.W. Beecher

Libraries are the wardrobes of literature, whence men, properly informed, may bring forth something for ornament, much for curiosity, and more for use.--Dyer

Let us pity those poor rich men who live barrenly in great bookless houses! Let us congratulate the poor that, in our day, books are so cheap that a man may every year add a hundred volumes to his library for the price of what his tobacco and beer would cost him. Among the earliest ambitions to be excited in clerks, workmen, journeymen, and, indeed, among all that are struggling up from nothing to something, is that of owning, and constantly adding to a library of good books. A little library, growing larger every year, is an honorable part of a young man's history. It is a man's duty to have books. A library is not a luxury, but one of the necessaries of life.--H.W. Beecher

From this slender beginning I have gradually formed a numerous and select library, the foundation of all my works, and the best comfort of my life, both at home and abroad.--Gibbon

My library was dukedom large enough.--Shakespeare

Consider what you have in the smallest chosen library. A company of the wisest and wittiest men that could be picked out of all civil countries, in a thousand years, have set in best order the results of their learning and wisdom. The men themselves were hid and inaccessible, solitary, impatient of interruption, fenced by etiquette; but the thought which they did not uncover to their bosom friend is here written out in transparent words to us, the strangers of another age. --Emerson

The true university of these days is a collection of books.--Carlyle

No possession can surpass, or even equal a good library, to the lover of books. Here are treasured up for his daily use and delectation, riches which increase by being consumed, and pleasures which never cloy.--J.A. Langford

What a world of wit is here packed together!--I know not whether the sight doth more dismay or comfort me.--It dismays me to think that here is so much I cannot know; it comforts me to think the this variety yields so good helps to know what I should.--Blessed be the memory of those who have left their blood, their spirits, their lives, in these precious books, and have willingly wasted themselves into these during monuments, to give light unto others.--Bp. Hall

A library may be regarded as the solemn chamber in which a man may take counsel with all who have been wise, and great, and good, and glorious among the men that have gone before him.--G. Dawson

The great consulting-room of a wise man is a library.--G. Dawson

Let every man, if possible, gather some good books under his roof, and obtain access for himself and family to some social library. Almost any luxury should be sacrificed to this.--William Ellery Channing

The first thing naturally when one enters a scholar's study or library, is to look at his books. One gets a notion very speedily of his tastes and the range of his pursuits by a glance round his bookshelves. --O.W. Holmes

A library is but the soul's burial ground.--H.W. Beecher

LINCOLN

...With malice toward none, with charity for all, with firmness in the right as God givesus to see the right, let us strive on to finish the work we are in; to bind up the Nation's wounds; to care for him who shall have borne the battle, and for his widow and his orphan--to do all which may achieve and cherish a just and lasting peace among ourselves and with all nations.--Abraham Lincoln

I know there is a God, and that He hates the injustice of slavery. I see the storm coming, and I know that His hand is in it. If He has a place and a work for me, and I think He has, I believe I am ready. I am nothing, but truth is everything. I know I am right, because I know that liberty is right, for Christ teaches it, and Christ is God.--Abraham Lincoln

I must confess that I am driven to my knees every day by the overwhelming conviction I have nowhere else to go. My wisdom and that of all about me is insufficient to meet the demands of the day. --Abraham Lincoln

When I came to Springfield, I was not a Christian. When I left Springfield for Washington and asked you to pray for me, I was not a Christian. When I received the bitterest blow of my life, the death of my son, I was not a Christian. When I went to Gettysburg, I was not a Christian. But there at Gettysburg I consecrated my heart to Christ.--Abraham Lincoln

LOVE

Love reads without letters and counts without arithmetic.--John Wanamaker

It is a beautiful necessity of our nature to love something.--Jerrold

The greatest pleasure of life is love.--Sir W. Temple

The heart of him who truly loves is a paradise on earth; he has God in himself, for God is love.--Lamennais

Love one human being purely and warmly, and you will love all. --The heart in this heaven, like the sun in its course, sees nothing, from the dewdrop to the ocean, but a mirror which it brightens, and warms, and fills.--Richter

Love gives itself; it is not bought.--Longfellow

That is the true season of love, when we believe that we alone can love, that no one could ever have loved so before us, and that no one will love in the same way after us.--Goethe

Love is never lost. If not reciprocated it will flow back and soften and purify the heart.--Washington Irving

Love is an image of God, and not a lifeless image, but the living essence of the divine nature which beams full of all goodness. --Luther

It is better to have loved and lost, than never to have loved at all. --Tennyson

We are shaped and fashioned by what we love.--Goethe

There is nothing holier in this life of ours than the first consciousness of love--the first fluttering of its silken wings--the first rising sound and breath of that wind which is so soon to sweep through the soul, to purify or to destroy.--Longfellow

Life is a flower of which love is the honey.--Victor Hugo

True love's the gift which God hath given, to man alone beneath the heaven. The silver link, the silver tie, which heart to heart, and mind to mind, in body and in soul can bind.--Walter Scott

Love never reasons, but profusely gives; gives, like a thoughtless prodigal, its all, and trembles then lest it has done too little.--Hannah Moore

Love is a thing to be *learned*. It is a difficult, complex maintenance of individual integrity throughout the incalculable processes of inter-human polarity.--D.H. Lawrence

I never could explain *why* I love anybody, or anything.--Walt Whitman

Love. . .is like a beautiful flower which I may not touch, but whose fragrance makes the garden a place of delight just the same.--Helen Keller

Love looks through a telescope; envy, through a microscope.--H.W. Shaw

The greatest happiness of life is the conviction that we are loved, loved for ourselves, or rather loved in spite of ourselves.--Victor Hugo

It is strange that men will talk of miracles, revelations, inspiration, and the like, as things past, while love remains.--Thoreau

Faith, like light, should always be simple and unbending; while love, like warmth, should beam forth on every side, and bend to every necessity of our brethren.--Luther

To love is to place our happiness in the happiness of another.--Leibnitz

A woman is more considerate in affairs of love than a man; because love is more the study and business of her life.--Washington Irving

Love needs new leaves every summer of life, as much as your elm tree, and new branches to grow broader and wider, and new flowers to cover the ground.--Mrs. Stowe

Love sees what no eye sees; love hears what no ear hears; and what never rose in the heart of man love prepares for its object.--Lavater

Not father or mother has loved you as God has, for it was that you might be happy He gave His only son.--When he bowed his head in the death hour, love solemnized its triumph; the sacrifice there was completed.--Longfellow

It is the duty of men to love even those who injure them.--Marcus Antoninus

If nobody loves you, be sure it is your own fault.--Doddridge

Love, it has been said, flows downward. The love of parents for their children has always been far more powerful than that of children for their parents; and who among the sons of men ever loved God with a thousandth part of the love which God has manifested to us?--Hare

Sweet is true love, though given in vain.--Tennyson

Love is indeed heaven upon earth; since heaven above would not be heaven without it; for where there is not love, there is fear; but, "Perfect love casteth out fear." And yet we naturally fear most to offend what we most love.--Penn

It is an old story, yet remains ever new.--Heinrich Heine

Love is the crowning grace of humanity, the holiest right of the soul, the golden link which binds us to duty and truth, the redeeming principle that chiefly reconciles the heart of life, and is prophetic of eternal good.--Petrarch

Mutual love, the crown of all our bliss.--Milton

Love understands love: it needs no talk.--F.R. Havergal

Love will find out the way.--Percy Reliques

Love can hope, where reason would despair.--Lyttleton

MOTIVE

There are possibilities below the threshold of our life which no one knows but God. We cannot understand ourselves or know the spring of our motives, consequently our examination of ourselves can never be unbiased or unprejudiced.--Chambers

Never fear to bring the sublimest motive to the smallest duty, and the most infinite comfort to the smallest trouble.--Phillips Brooks

Pure motives do not insure perfect results.--Bovee

In the motive lies the good or ill.--Dr. Johnson

Men's minds are as variant as their faces. Where the motives of their actions are pure, the operation of the former is no more to be imputed to them as a crime, than the appearance of the latter; for both, being the work of nature, are alike unavoidable.--George Washington

What makes life dreary is the want of motive.--George Eliot

He that does good for good's sake seeks neither praise nor reward, though sure of both at last.--William Penn

God made man to go by motives, and he will not go without them, any more than a boat without steam, or a balloon without gas.--H.W. Beecher

What society wants is a new motive, not a new cant.--Macaulay

MUSIC

Music is the mediator between the spiritual and the sensual life. Although the spirit be not master of that which it creates through music, yet it is blessed in this creation, which, like every creation of art, is mightier than the artist.--Beethoven

Let me have music dying, and I seek no more delight.--Keats

Music, in the best sense, does not require novelty; nay, the older it is, and the more we are accustomed to it, the greater its effect.--Goethe

There is something marvelous in music. I might almost say it is, in itself, a marvel. Its position is somewhere between the region of thought and that of phenomena; a glimmering medium between mind and matter, related to both and yet differing from either. Spiritual, and yet requiring rhythm; material, and yet independent of space.--H. Heine

Music resembles poetry; in each are numerous graces which no methods teach, and which a master hand alone can reach.--Pope

The man that hath not music in himself, and is not moved with concord of sweet sounds, is fit for treasons, stratagems, and spoils; let no man trust him.--Shakespeare

94

Music is the fourth great material want of our nature,--first food, then raiment, then shelter, then music.--Bovee

Music is a prophecy of what life is to be; the rainbow of promise translated out of seeing into hearing.--Mrs. L.M. Child

Music, of all the liberal arts, has the greatest influence over the passions, and is that to which the legislator ought to give the greatest encouragement.--Napoleon

It is in learning music that many youthful hearts learn to love. --Ricard

Next to theology I give to music the highest place and honor. And we see how David and all the saints have wrought their godly thoughts into verse, rhyme, and song.--Luther

The direct relation of music is not to ideas, but to emotions--in the works of its greatest masters, it is more marvelous, more mysterious than poetry.--Giles

Music washes away from the soul the dust of every-day life. --Auerbach

There is music in all things, if men had ears.--Byron

Lord, what music hast thou provided for thy saints in heaven, when thou affordest bad men such music on earth!--Izaak Walton

Music is the medicine of the breaking heart.--A. Hunt

Music is the child of prayer, the companion of religion. --Chateaubriand

I always loved music; whoso has skill in this art, is of a good temperament, fitted for all things. We must teach music in schools. A schoolmaster ought to have skill in music, or I would not regard him; neither should we ordain young men as preachers, unless they have been well exercised in music.--Martin Luther

Music wakes the soul, and lifts it high, and wings it with sublime desires, and fits it to bespeak the Deity.--Addison

Yea, music is the prophet's art; among the gifts that God hath sent, one of the most magnificent.--Longfellow

The meaning of song goes deep. Who is there that, in logical words, can express the effect music has on us? A kind of inarticulate, unfathomable speech, which leads us to the edge of the infinite, and lets us for moments gaze into that!--Carlyle

The hidden soul of harmony.--Milton

Music, if only listened to, and not scientifically cultivated, gives too much play to the feelings and fancy; the difficulties of the art draw forth the whole energies of the soul.--Richter

There is no feeling, perhaps, except the extremes of fear and grief, that does not find relief in music,--that does not make a man sing or play the better.--George Eliot

Music, among those who were styled the chosen people, was a religious art.--Addison

Men, even when alone, lighten their labors by song, however rude it may be.--Quintillian

Is there a heart that music cannot melt?--Beattie

Music cleanses the understanding, inspires it, and lifts it into a realm which it would not reach if it were left to itself.--H.W. Beecher

Music, when combined with a pleasurable idea, is poetry; music without the idea is simply music; the idea without the music is prose from its very definiteness.--Edgar Allen Poe

All musical people seem to be happy. It is the engrossing pursuit, --almost the only innocent and unpunished passion.--S. Smith

Music is not a science any more than poetry is. It is a sublime instinct, like genius of all kinds.--Ouida

I ever held this sentence of the poet as a cannon of my creed, "that whom God loveth not, they love not music."--T. Morley

Music when thus applied raises in the mind of the hearer great conceptions. It strengthens devotion, and advances praise into rapture. --Addison

Music,--we love it for the buried hopes, the garnered memories, the tender feelings it can summon at a touch.--L.E. Landon

Had I children, my utmost endeavors would be to make them musicians.--Horace Walpole

Music, of all the liberal arts, has the greatest influence over the passions, and is that to which the legislator ought to give the greatest encouragement.--Napoleon

Explain it as we may, a martial strain will urge a man into the front rank of battle sooner than an argument, and a fine anthem excite his devotion more certainly than a logical discourse.--Tuckerman

Let me die to the sounds of the delicious music.--Last words of Mirabeau

Music is the universal language of mankind.--Longfellow

Music is the only one of the fine arts in which not only man, but all other animals, have a common property,--mice and elephants, spiders and birds.--Richter

Music is the harmonious voice of creation, an echo of the invisible world, one not of the divine concord which the entire universe is destined one day to sound.--Mazzini

Music is the medicine of an afflicted mind, a sweet sad measure is the balm of a wounded spirit; and joy is heightened by exultant strains. --Henry Giles

Music is the art of the prophets, the only art that can calm the agitations of the soul; it is one of the most magnificent and delightful presents God has given us.--Luther

Music, once admitted to the soul, becomes a sort of spirit, and never dies. It wanders perturbedly through the halls and galleries of the memory, and is often heard again, distinct and living as when it first displaced the wavelets of the air.--Bulwer-Lytton

Those who love music are gentle and honest in their tempers. I always loved music, and would not, for a great matter, be without the little skill which I possess in the art.--Luther

Music is a sacred, a divine, a God-like thing, and was given to man by Christ to lift our hearts up to God, and make us feel something of the glory and beauty of God, and of all which God has made. --Charles Kingsley

And wheresoever, in his rich creation, Sweet music breathes-in wave, or bird, or soul--'Tis but the faint and far reverberation of that great tune to which the planets roll!--Frances S. Osgood

There let the pealing organ blow, to the full voiced quire below, in service high, and anthems clear, as may with sweetness, through mine ear, dissolve me into ecstasies, and bring all heaven before mine eyes.--Milton

Music the fiercest grief can charm, and fate's severest rage disarm. Music can soften pain to ease, and make despair and madness please; our joys below it can improve, and antedate the bliss above.--Pope

Of all the arts beneath the heaven, that man has found, or God has given, none draws the soul so sweet away, as music's melting, mystic lay; slight emblem of the bliss above, it soothes the spirit all to love.--Hogg

OBEDIENCE

To obey is better than sacrifice.--Bible

Obedience completes itself in understanding.--Phillips Brooks

Obedience is the mother of success.--AEschylus

To be a Christian is to obey Christ no matter how you feel.--H.W. Beecher

Obedience sums up our entire duty.--Hosea Ballou

Obedience is the key to every door.--George MacDonald

The first great law is to obey.--Schiller

The virtue of Christianity is obedience.--J.D. Hare

An obedient wife commands her husband.--Beaconsfield

I hourly learn a doctrine of obedience.--Shakespeare

I would rather obey than work miracles.--Luther

Obedience is the Christian's crown.--Schiller

We need only obey. There is guidance for each of us, and by lowly listening we shall hear the right word.--Emerson

Everywhere the flower of obedience is intelligence. Obey a man with cordial loyalty and you will understand him.--Phillips Brooks

Command is anxiety; obedience, easy.--Paley

Charms by accepting, by submitting sways, yet has her humor most when she obeys.--Pope

Woman's happiness consists in obeying; she objects to a man who yields too much.--Michelet

Let thy child's first lesson be obedience, and the second will be what thou wilt.--Benjamin Franklin

Women are perfectly well aware that the more they seem to obey the more they rule.--Michelet

Love naturally reverses the idea of obedience, and causes the struggle between any two who truly love each other to be, not who shall command, but who shall yield.--Frances Power Cobbe

All the good of which humanity is capable is comprised in obedience.--J. Stuart Mill

I find the doing of the will of God leaves me no time for disputing about His plans.--George MacDonald

It is foolish to strive with what we cannot avoid; we are born subjects, and to obey God is perfect liberty; he that does this shall be free, safe and quiet; all his actions shall succeed to his wishes.--Seneca

That was a judicious mother who said, "I obey my children for the first year of their lives, but ever after I expect them to obey me." --H.W. Beecher

He praiseth God best that serveth and obeyeth Him most; the life of thankfulness consists in the thankfulness of the life.--Burkitt

The history of all the great characters of the Bible is summed up in this one sentence: They acquainted themselves with God, and acquiesced in His will in all things.--Richard Cecil

Obedience insures greatness, whilst disobedience leads to a repulse. Whosoever possesseth the qualities of righteousness placeth his head on the threshold of obedience.--Saadi

How will you find good? It is not a thing of choice; it is a river that flows from the foot of the Invisible Throne and flows by the path of obedience.--George Eliot

As unto the bow the string is, so unto the man is woman; though she bends him, she obeys him; though she draws him, yet she follows, --useless each without the other.--Longfellow

Women never really command until they have given their promise to obey; and they are never in more danger of being made slaves than when the men are at their feet.--Farquhar

Obedience alone gives the right to command.--Emerson

Heaven doth divide, the state of man in divers functions, setting endeavor in continual motion; to which is fix'd, an aim or butt, Obedience.--Shakespeare

Light is a special help to obedience, and obedience is a singular help to increase light.--Flavel

Be it remembered that we command nature, as it were, by obeying nature's laws; so the woman who would control her husband does so through obedience.--Haliburton

Let the ground of all thy religious actions be obedience; examine not why it is commanded, but observe it because it is commanded. True obedience neither procrastinates nor questions.--Francis Quarles

Obedience is our universal duty and destiny; wherein whoso will not bend must break; too early and too thoroughly we cannot be trained to know the "would," in this world of ours, is a mere zero to "should," and for most part as the smallest of fractions even to "shall."--Carlyle

Obedience is, indeed, founded on a kind of freedom, else it would become mere subjugation, but that freedom is only granted that obedience may be more perfect; and thus while a measure of license is necessary to exhibit the individual energies of things, the fairness and pleasantness and perfection of them all consist in their restraint. --Ruskin

O Lord, who art our guide even unto death, grant us, I pray Thee, grace to follow Thee withersoever Thou goest. In little daily duties to which Thou callest us, bow down our wills to simple obedience. --Christina G. Rossetti

Obedience, we may remember, is a part of religion, and therefore an element of peace; but love which includes obedience is the whole. --George Sewell

I believe that the fewer the laws in a home the better; but there is one law which should be as plainly understood as the shining of the sun is visible at noonday, and that is, implicit and instantaneous obedience from the child to the parent, not only for the peace of the home, but for the highest good of the child.--A.E. Kittredge

The first law that ever God gave to man was a law of pure obedience; it was a commandment naked and simple, wherein man had nothing to inquire after, or to dispute, forasmuch as to obey is the proper office of a rational soul, acknowledging a heavenly superior and benefactor. From obedience and submission spring all other virtues, as all sin does from self-opinion.--Montaigne

Obey thy parents; keep thy word justly; swear not.--Shakespeare

Look carefully that love to God and obedience to His commands be the principle and spring from whence thy actions flow; and that the glory of God and the salvation of thy soul be the end to which all thy actions tend; and that the word of God be thy rule and guide in every enterprise and undertaking. "As many as walk by his rule, peace be unto them, and mercy."--Burkitt

OPPORTUNITY

You can never ride on the wave that came in and went out yesterday.
--John Wanamaker

Chance opportunities make us known to others, and still more to ourselves.--Rochefoucauld

The secret of success in life, is for a man to be ready for his opportunity when it comes.--Disraeli

Great opportunities come to all, but many do not know they have met them.--The only preparation to take advantage of them, is simple fidelity to what each day brings.--A.E. Dunning

A wise man will make more opportunities than he finds.--Bacon

Vigilance in watching opportunity; tact and daring in seizing upon opportunity; force and persistence in crowding opportunity to its utmost of possible achievement--these are the martial virtues which must command success.--Austin Phelps

For truth and duty it is ever the fitting time; who waits until circumstances completely favor his undertaking, will never accomplish anything.--Luther

Next to knowing when to seize an opportunity, the most important thing in life is to know when to forego an advantage.--Disraeli

Who seeks, and will not take when once 'tis offered, shall never find it more.--Shakespeare

ORATORY

The passions are the only orators that always succeed. They are, as it were, nature's art of eloquence, fraught with infallible rules. Simplicity, with the aid of the passions, persuades more than the utmost eloquence without it.--Rochefoucauld

It is the first rule in oratory that a man must appear such as he would persuade others to be; and that can be accomplished only by the force of his life.--Swift

There is not power like that of true oratory. Caesar controlled men by exciting their fears; Cicero, by captivating their affections and swaying their passions. The influence of the one perished with its author; that of the other continues to this day.--Henry Clay

What too many orators want in depth, they give you in length. --Montesquieu

In oratory, the greatest art is to conceal art.--Swift

An orator without judgment is a horse without a bridle. --Theoprastus

Orators are most vehement when they have the weakest cause, as men get on horseback when they cannot walk.--Cicero

Extemporaneous speaking is, indeed, the groundwork of the orator's art; preparation is the last finish, and the most difficult of all his accomplishments. To learn by heart as a schoolboy, or to prepare as an orator, are two things, not only essentially different, but essentially antagonistic to each other; for the work most opposed to an effective oration is an elegant essay.--Bulwer

Eloquence is vehement simplicity.--Cecil

An orator or author is never successful till he has learned to make his words smaller than his ideas.--Emerson

Oratory is the power of beating down your adversary's arguments and putting better in their place.--Johnson

Oratory, like the drama, abhors lengthiness; like the drama it must keep doing. It avoids, as frigid, prolonged metaphysical soliloquy. Beauties themselves, if they delay or distract the effect which should be produced on the audience, become blemishes.--Bulwer-Lytton

The language of the heart--the language which "comes from the heart" and "goes to the heart"--is always simple, always graceful, and always full of power, but no art of rhetoric can teach it. It is at once the easiest and most difficult language--difficult, since it needs a heart to speak it, easy, because its periods though rounded and full of harmony, are still unstudied.--Bovee

Every man should study conciseness in speaking; it is a sign of ignorance not to know that long speeches, though they may please the speaker, are the torture of the hearer.--Feltham

There is no true orator who is not a hero.--Emerson

The object of oratory alone is not truth, but persuasion.--Macaulay

Those orators who give us much noise and many words, but little argument and less wit, and who are the loudest when least lucid, should take a lesson from the great volume of nature; she often gives us the lightning without the thunder, but never the thunder without the lightning.--Burritt

PATIENCE

Everything comes if a man will only wait.--Tancred

To know how to wait is the great secret of success.--De Maistre

Patient waiting is often the highest way of doing God's will.--Collier

How poor are they who have not patience! What wound did ever heal but by degrees.--Shakespeare

Patience is the art of hoping.--Vauvenargues

Patience is not passive: on the contrary it is active; it is concentrated strength. There is one form of hope which is never unwise, and which certainly does not diminish with the increase of knowledge. In that form it changes its name, and we call it patience.--Bulwer-Lytton

The two powers which in my opinion constitute a wise man are those of bearing and forbearing.--Epictetus

All that I have accomplished, or expect or hope to accomplish, has been and will be by that plodding, patient, persevering process of accretion which builds the ant-heap, particle by particle, thought by thought, fact by fact.--Elihu Burritt

Never think that God's delays are God's denials. Hold on; hold fast; hold out.--Patience is genius.--Buffon

There is no such thing as preaching patience into people unless the sermon is so long that they have to practice it while they hear. No man can learn patience except by going out into the hurly-burly world, and taking life just as it blows.--Patience is but lying to and riding out the gale.--H.W. Beecher

Patience and time do more than strength or passion.--La Fontaine

It is not necessary for all men to be great in action. The greatest and sublimest power is often simple patience.--Horace Bushnell

Patience is bitter, but its fruit is sweet.--Rousseau

Patience! Why, it is the soul of peace; of all the virtues, it is nearest kin to heaven; it makes men look like gods. The best of men that ever wore earth about him was a sufferer,--a soft, meek, patient, humble, tranquil spirit; the first true gentleman that ever breathed.--Decker

Patience is so like fortitude that she seems either her sister or her daughter.--Aristotle

Patience is the courage of the conqueror, the strength of man against destiny--of the one against the world, and of the soul against matter. --Therefore it is the courage of the gospel; and its importance, in a social view and to races and institutions, cannot be too earnestly inculcated.--Bulwer-Lytton

What I have done is due to patient thought.--Sir Isaac Newton

He surely is most in need of another's patience, who has none of his own.--Lavater

Patience and fortitude conquer all things.--Emerson

To endure is greater than to dare.--Thackeray

Patience is the ballast of the soul, that will keep it from rolling and tumbling in the greatest storms; and he that will venture out without this to make him sail even and steady will certainly make shipwreck and drown himself, first in the cares and sorrows of this world, and then in perdition.--Bishop Hopkins

Patient endurance is Godlike--Longfellow

Patience is a necessary ingredient of genius.--Disraeli

There are times when patience proves at fault.--Robert Browning

In your patience ye are strong.--Miss Barrett

He that can have patience can have what he will.--Franklin

PATRIOTISM

The noblest motive is the public good.--Virgil

Be just and fear not; let all the ends thou aimest at, be thy country's, thy God's, and truth's.--Shakespeare

Let our object be our country, our whole country, and nothing but our country. And, by the blessing of God, may that country itself become a vast and splendid monument, not of oppression and terror, but of wisdom, of peace, and of liberty, upon which the world may gaze with admiration forever.--Daniel Webster

National enthusiasm is the great nursery of genius.--Tuckerman

Had I a dozen sons--each in my love alike,--I had rather have eleven die nobly for their country, than one voluptuously surfeit out of action.--Shakespeare

Whene'er our country calls, friends, sons, and sires should yield their treasure up, nor own a sense beyond the public safety.--Brooke

There can be no affinity nearer than our country.--Plato

Of the whole sum of human life no small part is that which consists of a man's relations to his country, and his feelings concerning it. --Gladstone

The love of country produces good manners; and good manners, love of country.--The less we satisfy our individual passions, the more we leave to our general.--Montesquieu

I have heard something said about allegiance to the south: I know no south, no north, no east, no west, to which I owe any allegiance. --Henry Clay

I do love my country's good with a respect more tender, more holy and profound than mine own life.--Shakespeare

My country claims me all, claims every passion, her liberty henceforth be all my thought, for her, my life, I'd willingly resign, and say with transport that the gain was mine.--Martyn

Liberty and union, now and forever, one and inseparable.--Daniel Webster

Our country's welfare is our first concern, and who promotes that best, best proves his duty.--Havard

Love of country is one of the loftiest virtues; and so treason against it has been considered among the most damning sins.--E.A. Storrs

I hope to find my country in the right; however, I will stand by her, right or wrong.--J.J. Crittenden

"Shoot, if you must, this old gray head, but spare your country's flag," she said.--Whittier

I was born an American; I live an American; I shall die an American! --Daniel Webster

If anyone attempts to haul down the American flag, shoot him on the spot.--John A. Dix

I only regret that I have but one life to lose for my country.--Nathan Hale

We join ourselves to no party that does not carry the flag and keep step to the music of the Union.--Rufus Choate

We mutually pledge to each other our lives, our fortunes, and our sacred honor.--Jefferson

The man who loves home best, and loves it most unselfishly, loves his country best.--J.G. Holland

One flag, one land, one heart, one hand, One Nation evermore!
--Holmes

. . .This nation, under God, shall have a new birth of freedom, and
that government of the people, by the people, for the people, shall not
perish from the earth.--Abraham Lincoln

This is a maxim which I have received by hereditary tradition, not
only from my father, but also from my grandfather and his ancestors,
that after what I owe to God, nothing should be more dear or more
sacred than the love and respect I owe to my country.--De Thou

I am not a Virginian, but an American.--Patrick Henry

There are no points of the compass on the chart of true patriotism.
--Robt. C. Winthrop

The mystic chords of memory, stretching from every battlefield and
patriot grave to every living heart and hearthstone all over this broad
land, will yet swell the chorus of the Union, when again touched, as
surely they will be, by the better angels of our nature.--Abraham
Lincoln

That is a true sentiment which makes us feel that we do not love our
country less, but more, because we have laid up in our minds the
knowledge of other lands and other institutions and other races, and
have had enkindled afresh within us the instinct of a common
humanity, and of the universal beneficence of the Creator.--Dean
Stanley

It should be the work of a genuine and noble patriotism to raise the
life of the nation to the level of its privileges; to harmonize its general practice with its abstract principles; to reduce to actual facts the
ideals of its institutions; to elevate instruction into knowledge; to
deepen knowledge into wisdom; to render knowledge and wisdom
complete in righteousness; and to make the love of country perfect in
the love of man.--Henry Giles

He who loathes war, and will do everything in his power to avert it,
but who will, in the last extremity, encounter its perils, from love of
country and of home--who is willing to sacrifice himself and all that
is dear to him in life, to promote the well-being of his fellow-man,
will ever receive a worthy homage.--Abbott

It is sweet and glorious to die for one's country.--Horace

PEACE

Peace does not dwell in outward things, but within the soul; we may preserve it in the midst of the bitterest pain, if our will remain firm and submissive. Peace in this life springs from acquiescence, not in an exemption from suffering.--Fenelon

Peace rules the day, where reason rules the mind.--Collins

The source of peace is God, not myself; it never is my peace but always His, and if once He withdraws, it is not there.--Oswald Chambers

Five great enemies to peace inhabit with us: viz., avarice, ambition, envy, anger, and pride. If those enemies were to be banished, we should infallibly enjoy perpetual peace.--Petrarch

If we have not peace within ourselves, it is in vain to seek it from outward sources.--Rouchefoucauld.

Lovely concord and most sacred peace doth nourish virtue, and fast friendship breed.--Spenser

We love peace, but not peace at any price.--There is a peace more destructive of the manhood of living man, than war is destructive of his body.--Chains are worse than bayonets.--Jerrold

Nothing can bring you peace but yourself; nothing can bring you peace but the triumph of principles.--Emerson

To be prepared for war is one of the most effectual means of preserving peace.--Washington

I am a man of peace. God knows how I love peace. But I hope I shall never be such a coward as to mistake oppression for peace.--Kossuth

The Pilgrim they laid in a large upper chamber, whose window opened toward the sun-rising; the name of the chamber was Peace, where he slept till break of day, and then he awoke and sang. --Bunyan

Speak, move, act in peace, as if you were in prayer. In truth, this is prayer.--Fenelon

People are always expecting to get peace in heaven; but you know whatever peace they get there will be ready-made. What ever of making peace they can be blest for must be on the earth here.--Ruskin

Peace is rarely denied to the peaceful.--Schiller

Peace is the fairest form of happiness.--William Ellery Channing

As on the sea of Galilee the Christ is whispering "Peace!"--Whittier

Peace is liberty in tranquillity.--Cicero

Thy peace shall be in much patience.--Thomas a Kempis

You may assuredly find perfect peace, if you are resolved to do that which your Lord has plainly required--and content that He should indeed require no more of you--than to do justice, to love mercy, and to walk humbly with Him.--John Ruskin

Peace won by compromise is usually a short-lived achievement. --Winfield Scott

They shall beat their swords into ploughshares, and their spears into pruning hooks; nation shall not lift up sword against nation, neither shall they learn war any more.--Bible

I have never advocated war, except as a means of peace.--U.S. Grant

How different the peace of God from that of the world! It calms the passions, preserves the purity of conscience, is inseparable from righteousness, unites us to God and strengthens us against temptations. The peace of the soul consists in an absolute resignation to the will of God.--Fenelon

No peace was ever won from fate by subterfuge or argument; no peace is ever in store for any of us, but that which we shall win by victory over shame or sin--victory over the sin that oppresses, as well as over that which corrupts.--Ruskin

Even peace may be purchased at too high a price.--Franklin

Blessedness is promised to the peacemaker, not to the conqueror.
--Quarles

All things that speak of heaven speak of peace.--Bailey

PERSEVERANCE

Overcome a hard job, overcome a difficult and discouraging job;
fight, fight, fight, never stop!--John Wanamaker

Every noble work is at first impossible.--Carlyle

There are two ways of attaining an important end--force and perseverance. Force falls to the lot only of the privileged few, but austere
and sustained perseverance can be practiced by the most insignificant. Its silent power grows irresistible with time.--Mad. Swetchine

The conditions of conquest are always easy. We have but to toil
awhile, endure awhile, believe always, and never turn back.--Simms

I hold a doctrine, to which I owe not much, indeed, but all the little I
ever had, namely, that with ordinary talent and extraordinary perseverance, all things are attainable.--T.F. Buxton

The nerve that never relaxes, the eye that never blenches, the thought
that never wanders--these are the masters of victory.--Burke

Victory belongs to the most persevering.--Napoleon

Never despair; but if you do, work on in despair.--Burke

Perseverance is king.--H.W. Shaw

Press on! a better fate awaits thee.--Victor Hugo

Hope against hope, and ask till ye receive.--Montgomery

Whoever perseveres will be crowned.--Herder

A falling drop at last will carve a stone.--Lucretius

It is all very well to tell me that a young man has distinguished himself by a brilliant first speech. He may go on, or he may be satisfied with his first triumph; but show me a young man who has not succeeded at first, and nevertheless has gone on, and I will back that young man to do better than most of those who have succeeded at the first trial.--Charles James Fox

Hard pounding, gentlemen; but we will see who can pound the longest.--Wellington

No rock so hard but that a little wave may beat admission in a thousand years.--Tennyson

Great works are performed not by strength but by perseverance. --Johnson

I'm proof against that word "Failure." I've seen behind it. The only failure a man ought to fear is failure in cleaving to the purpose he sees to be best.--George Eliot

Those who would attain to any marked degree of excellence in a chosen pursuit must work, and work hard for it, prince or peasant. --Bayard Taylor

Great effects come of industry and perseverance; for audacity doth almost bind and mate the weaker sort of minds.--Bacon

Life affords no higher pleasure than that of surmounting difficulties, passing from one step of success to another, forming new wishes and seeing them gratified. He that labors in any great or laudable undertaking has his fatigues first supported by hope and afterwards rewarded by joy.--Dr. Johnson

If there be one thing on earth which is truly admirable, it is to see God's wisdom blessing an inferiority of natural powers, where they have been honestly, truly, and zealously cultivated.--Dr. Arnold
The block of granite, which was an obstacle in the pathway of the weak, becomes a stepping-stone in the pathway of the stone.--Carlyle

By gnawing through a dyke even a rat may drown a nation.--Edward Burke

The virtue lies in the struggle, not the prize.--R.M. Milnes

Did you ever hear of a man who had striven all his life faithfully and singly towards an object, and in no measure obtained it? If a man constantly aspires, is he not elevated? Did ever a man try heroism, magnanimity, truth, sincerity, and find that there was not advantage in them--that it was a vain endeavor?--Thoreau

Much rain wears the marble.--Shakespeare

PLANNING

What's the use of a plan if we do not work it?--John Wanamaker

What is a plan? A plan is a method of action, procedure, or arrangement. It is a program to be done. It is a design to carry into effect, an idea, a thought, a project, or a development. Therefore, a plan is a concrete means to help you fulfill your desires.--Earl Prevette

The air is full of plans--and the plans are full of air.--John Wanamaker

Plans get you into things but you got to work your way out.--Will Rogers

Make big plans, but change your plans as time changes.--Marchant
The most effective way to live reasonably is every morning to make a plan of one's day and every night to examine the results obtained. --Alexis Carrel

PRAISE

There is not a person we employ who does not, like ourselves, desire recognition, praise, gentleness, forbearance, patience.--H.W. Beecher

We are all excited by the love of praise, and it is the noblest spirits that feel it most.--Cicero

One of the most essential preparations for eternity is delight in praising God; a higher acquirement, I do think, than even delight and devotedness in prayer.--Chalmers

The sweetest of all sounds is praise.--Xenophon

Among the smaller duties of life, I hardly know any one more important than that of not praising where praise is not due. Reputation is one of the prizes for which men contend: it produces more labor and more talent than twice the wealth of a country could ever rear up. It is the coin of genius, and it is the imperious duty of every man to bestow it with the most scrupulous justice and the wisest economy. --Sydney Smith

As the Greek said, many men know how to flatter; few know to praise.--Wendell Phillips

Praise is the best auxiliary to prayer.--He who most bears in mind what has been done for him by God will be most emboldened to ask for fresh gifts from above.--H. Melville

Praise, like gold and diamonds, owes its value only to its scarcity. It becomes cheap as it becomes vulgar, and will no longer raise expectation or animate enterprise.--Johnson

Praise follows truth afar off, and only overtakes her at the grave; plausibility clings to her skirts and holds her back till then.--J.R. Lowell

It is no flattery to give a friend a due character; for commendation is as much the duty of a friend as reprehension.--Plutarch

The praises of others may be of use in teaching us, not what we are, but what we ought to be.--Hare

It takes a great deal of grace to be able to bear praise. Censure seldom does us much hurt. A man struggles up against slander, and the discouragement which comes of it may not be an unmixed evil; but praise soon suggests pride, and is therefore not an unmixed good. --Spurgeon

Thank not those faithful who praise all thy words and actions, but those who kindly reprove thy faults.--Socrates

Praise, more divine than prayer; prayer points our ready path to heaven; praise is already there.--Young

A man who does not love praise is not a full man.--H.W. Beecher

Let everything that hath breath praise the Lord.--Bible

Praise undeserved is satire in disguise.--Broadhurst

Good things should be praised.--Shakespeare

He hurts me most who lavishly commends.--Churchill

Praise consists in the love of God, in wonder at the goodness of God, in recognition of the gifts of God, in seeing God in all things He gives us, aye, and even in the things that He refuses to us; so as to see our whole life in the light of God; and seeing this, to bless Him, adore Him, and glorify Him.--Manning

His praise is lost who waits till all commend.--Pope

Praise is the best diet for us, after all.--Sydney Smith

He who praises everybody praises nobody.--Johnson

Those who are greedy of praise prove that they are poor in merit. --Plutarch

When thou receivest praise, take it indifferently, and return it to God, the giver of the gift, or blesser of the action.--Jeremy Taylor

You may be liberal in your praise where praise is due: it costs nothing; it encourages much.--Horace Mann

We are all excited by the love of praise, and the noblest are most influenced by glory.--Cicero

As the Greek said, "Many men know how to flatter, few men know how to praise."--Wendell Phillips

PRAYER

Prayer will not equip us for greater works, prayer is the greater work.--Oswald Chambers

He who runs from God in the morning will scarcely find Him in the rest of the day.--Bunyan

Prayer is not in itself meritorious. It lays God under no obligation nor puts Him in debt to any. He hears prayer because He is good, and for no other reason. Nor is faith meritorious; it is simply confidence in the goodness of God, and the lack of it is a reflection upon God's holy character.--A.B. Tozer

The fewer words the better prayer.--Luther

I have been driven many times to my knees by the overwhelming conviction that I had nowhere else to go. My own wisdom, and that of all about me, seemed insufficient for the day.--Abraham Lincoln

One of the most essential preparations for eternity is delight in praising God; a higher acquirement, I do think, than even delight and devotedness in prayer.--Chalmers

God hears a woman's prayers, I believe, before He hears any other. --John Wanamaker

Prayer is a sincere, sensible, affectionate pouring out of the soul to God, through Christ, in the strength and assistance of the Spirit, for such things as God has promised.--Bunyan

Prayer is not overcoming God's reluctance; it is laying hold of His highest willingness.--Trench

The body of our prayer is the sum of our duty; and as we must ask of God whatsoever we need, so we must watch and labor for all that we ask.--Jeremy Taylor

Certain thoughts are prayers. There are moments when, whatever be the attitude of the body, the soul is on its knees.--Victor Hugo

Every good and holy desire, though it lack the form, hath in itself the substance and force of a prayer with God, who regardeth the very moanings, groans, and sighings of the heart.--Hooker

The prayer that begins with trustfulness, and passes on into waiting, will always end in thankfulness, triumph, and praise.--A. Maclaren

If a man will just set his heart down on its knees, he will find that there is an awful lot that he does not need to know to receive Jesus Christ!--A.B. Tozer

Our prayers should be for blessings in general, for God knows best what is good for us.--Socrates

Prayer is not eloquence, but earnestness; not the definition of help-lessness, but the feeling of it; not figures of speech, but earnestness of soul.--H. More

A prayer in its simplest definition is merely a wish turned God-ward.--Phillips Brooks

We should pray with as much earnestness as those who expect every-thing from God; and should act with as much energy as those who expect everything from themselves.--Colton

Prayer covers the whole of a man's life. There is no thought, feeling, yearning, or desire, however low, trifling, or vulgar we may deem it, which, if it affects our real interest or happiness, we may not lay before God and be sure of his sympathy. His nature is such that our often coming does not tire him. The whole burden of the whole life of every man may be rolled on to God and not weary Him, though it has wearied the man.--H.W. Beecher

They never sought in vain that sought the Lord aright.--Burns

Any heart turned God-ward, feels more joy in one short hour of prayer, than e'er was raised by all the feasts on earth since its foun-dation.--Bailey

The deepest wishes of the heart find expression in secret prayer.
--George E. Rees

Prayer without watching is hypocrisy; and watching without prayer is presumption.--W. Jay

Let us pray! God is just, he tries us; God is pitiful, he will comfort us; let us pray!--Joseph Roux

True prayer is only another name for the love of God. Its excellence does not consist in the multitude of our words; for our Father knoweth what things we have need of before we ask Him. The true prayer is that of the heart, and the heart prays only for what it desires. To pray, then, is to desire--but to desire what God would have us desire.--Fenelon

117

Oh, happy vantage of a kneeling knee!--Shakespeare

No man ever prayed heartily without learning something.--Emerson

In prayer it is better to have a heart without words, than words without a heart.--Bunyan

He that will learn to pray, let him go to sea.--Herbert

Battering the gates of heaven with storms of prayer.--Tennyson

Prayer is the breath of a new-born soul, and there can be no Christian life without it.--Rowland Hill

Prayer is a powerful thing; for God has bound and tied himself thereunto.--Martin Luther

Prayers are heard in heaven very much in proportion to our faith. Little faith will get very great mercies, but great faith still greater. --Spurgeon

Prayer is a shield to the soul, a sacrifice to God, and a scourge for Satan.--Bunyan

Ye ask, and receive not, because ye ask amiss.--Bible

He that loveth little prayeth little; he that loveth much prayeth much.--St. Augustine

Sometimes a fog will settle over a vessel's deck and yet leave the top-mast clear. Then a sailor goes up aloft and gets a lookout which the helmsman on deck cannot get. So prayer sends the soul aloft; lifts it above the clouds in which our selfishness and egotism befog us, and gives us a chance to see which way to steer.--C.H. Spurgeon

PREACHING

Though we live in a reading age and in a reading community, yet the preaching of the Gospel is the form in which human agency has been and still is most efficaciously employed for the spiritual improvement of men.--Daniel Webster

The life of a pious minister is visible rhetoric.--Hooker

Don't's and Do's about Texts: Don't be Clever. Don't be Controversial. Don't be Conceited. Do be Careful. Do be Consecrated. Do be Concentrated.--Oswald Chambers

Send your audience away with a desire for, and an impulse toward spiritual improvement, or your preaching will be a failure. --Goulburn

It requires as much reflection and wisdom to know what is not to be put into a sermon, as what is.--Cecil

The Christian ministry is the worst of all trades, but the best of all professions.--John Newton

For years I have attended the ministrations of the house of God on the Sabbath, and though my pursuits are literary, I tell you I have received through all these years, more intellectual nourishment and stimulus from the pulpit, than from all other sources combined.--J.G. Holland

A popular preacher once said of his pulpit efforts, "I always roar when I have nothing to say."

It is not a minister's wisdom but his conviction which imparts itself to others. Nothing gives life but life. Real flame alone kindles other flame; this was the power of the apostles: "We believe and therefore speak." Firm faith in what they spoke, that was the basis of the apostles strength.--F.W. Robertson

A preacher should have the skill to teach the unlearned simply, roundly, and plainly; for teaching is of more importance than exhorting.--Luther

I don't like those mighty fine preachers who round off their sentences so beautifully that they are sure to roll off the sinner's conscience. --Rowland Hill

As the great test of medical practice is that it heals the patient, so the great test of preaching is that it converts and builds up the hearers. --H.L. Wayland

The world looks at ministers out of the pulpit to know what they mean when in it.--Cecil

That is not the best sermon which makes the hearers go away talking to one another, and praising the speaker, but which makes them go away thoughtful and serious, and hastening to be alone.--Bp. Burnet

Preaching from prejudice is dangerous, it makes a man dogmatic and certain that he is right.--Oswald Chambers

I would have every minister of the Gospel address his audience with the zeal of a friend, with the generous energy of a father, and with the exuberant affection of a mother.--Fenelon

To preach more than half an hour, a man should be an angel himself or have angels for hearers.--Whitefield

Some plague the people with too long sermons; for the faculty of listening is a tender thing, and soon becomes weary and satiated. --Luther

He who the sword of heaven will bear, should be as holy as severe. --Shakespeare

Many a meandering discourse one hears, in which the preacher aims at nothing, and hits it.--Whately

I love a serious preacher, who speaks for my sake and not for his own; who seeks my salvation, and not his own vainglory. He best deserves to be heard who uses speech only to clothe his thoughts, and his thoughts only to promote truth and virtue. Nothing is more detestable than a professed declaimer, who retails his discourses as a quack does his medicine.--Massillon

My grand point in preaching is to break the hard heart, and to heal the broken one.--John Newton

All things with which we deal preach to us. What is a farm but a mute Gospel! The chaff and the wheat, weeds and plants, blight, rain, insects, sun,--it is a sacred emblem from the first furrow of spring to the last stack which the snow of winter overtakes in the fields.--Emerson

Genius is not essential to good preaching, but a live man is.--A. Phelps

The world is dying for want, not of good preaching, but of good hearing.--G.D. Boardman

A minister without boldness is like a smooth file, a knife without an edge, a sentinel that is afraid to let off his gun. If men will be bold in sin, ministers must be bold to reprove.--Gurnall

A good discourse is that from which one can take nothing without taking the life.--Fenelon

Evil ministers of good things, says Hooker, are like torches, a light to others, but not to themselves, or, as Cox says, like Noah's carpenters, building an ark for others, while they themselves are not saved by it.

I preached as never sure to preach again, and as a dying man to dying men.--Baxter

Of Bradford's preaching, Foxe says, "Sharply he opened and reproved sin; sweetly he preached Christ crucified; pithily he impugned heresy and error; and earnestly he persuaded to a godly life."

To love to preach is one thing--to love those to whom we preach, quite another.--Cecil

No sermon is of any value, or likely to be useful, which has not the three R's in it; ruin by the fall, redemption by Christ, and regeneration by the Holy Spirit.--My aim in every sermon, is loudly to call sinners, to quicken saints, and to be made a blessing to all.--Ryland

PRIDE

Pride, the first peer and president of hell.--Defoe

There is no better way to keep God out of your soul than to be full of self.--Fulton Sheen

Pride, like the magnet, constantly points to one object, self, but unlike the magnet, it has no attractive pole, but at all points repels.--Cotton

Pride, the most dangerous of all faults, proceeds from want of sense, or want of thought.--Dillon

The devil did grin, for his darling sin is pride that apes humility. --Coleridge

If a proud man makes me keep my distance, the comfort is that he keeps his at the same time.--Swift

Of all the causes which conspire to blind man's erring judgment, and mislead the mind, what the weak head with strongest bias rules, is pride--that never failing vice of fools.--Pope

The only reason I can't get to God is pride, no matter how humble I seem.--Oswald Chambers

If a man has a right to be proud of anything, it is of a good action done as it ought to be, without any base interest lurking at the bottom of it.--Sterne

None have more pride than those who dream that they have none. You may labor against vainglory till you conceive that you are humble, and the fond conceit of your humility will prove to be pride in full bloom.--Spurgeon

A proud man is seldom a grateful man, for he never thinks he gets as much as he deserves.--H.W. Beecher

John Bunyan had a great dread of spiritual pride; and once, after he had preached a very fine sermon, and his friends crowded round to shake him by the hand, while they expressed the utmost admiration of his eloquence, he interrupted them, saying: "Ay! you need not remind me of that, for the Devil told me of it before I was out of the pulpit!"--Southey

You who are ashamed of your poverty, and blush for your calling, are a snob; as are you who boast of your pedigree, or are proud of your wealth.--Thackeray

Every proud person takes himself too seriously.--Fulton Sheen

Let me give you the history of pride in three small chapters. The beginning of pride was in heaven. The continuance of pride is on earth. The end of pride is in hell. This history shows how unprofitable it is.--R. Newton

Pride breakfasted with plenty, dined with poverty, and supped with infamy.--Franklin

PRINCIPLES

Important principles may and must be flexible.--Abraham Lincoln

Our principles are the springs of our actions; our actions, the springs of our happiness or misery. Too much care, therefore, cannot be taken in forming our principles.--Skelton

What is the essence and the life of character? Principle, integrity, independence, or, as one of our great old writers has it, "That inbred loyalty unto virtue which can serve her without a livery."--Bulwer-Lytton

Principle is a passion for truth and right.--Hazlitt

Expedients are for the hour; principles for the ages.--H.W. Beecher

Many men do not allow their principles to take root, but pull them up every now and then, as children do the flowers they have planted, to see if they are growing.--Longfellow

Always vote for a principle, though you vote alone, and you may cherish the sweet reflection that your vote is never lost.--John Quincy Adams

Principles last forever; but special rules pass away with the things and conditions to which they refer.--Seeley

Back of every noble life there are principles which have fashioned it. --G.H. Lorimer

PROFANITY

Most people who commit a sin count on some personal benefit to be derived therefrom, but profanity has not even this excuse.--Hosea Ballou

Nothing is a greater sacrilege than to prostitute the great name of God to the petulancy of an idle tongue.--J. Taylor

A single profane expression betrays a man's low breeding.--Joseph Cook

It is difficult to account for a practice which gratifies no passion and promotes no interest.--Robert Hall

The General is sorry to be informed that the foolish and wicked practice of profane cursing and swearing, a vice hitherto little known in an American army, is growing into fashion. He hopes the officers will, by example as well as in influence, endeavor to check it, and that both they and the men will reflect that we can have little hope of the blessing of heaven on our arms, if we insult it by our impiety and folly. Added to this, it is a vice so mean and low, without any temptation, that every man of sense and character detests and despises it. --Washington

Profaneness is a brutal vice. He who indulges in it is no gentleman, I care not what his stamp may be in society; I care not what clothes he wears, or what culture he boasts.--Chapin

PROSPERITY

It is poor prosperity that is blind to the need of God's favor.--John Wanamaker

Everything in the world may be endured, except continual prosperity.--Goethe

Prosperity is the touchstone of virtue; for it is less difficult to bear misfortunes than to remain uncorrupted by pleasure.--Tacitus

If adversity hath killed his thousands, prosperity hath killed his ten thousands; therefore adversity is to be preferred. The one deceives, the other instructs; the one is miserably happy, the other happily miserable; and therefore many philosophers have voluntarily sought adversity and commend it in their receipts.--Burton

Prosperity has this property, it puffs up narrow souls, makes them imagine themselves high and mighty, and looks down upon the world with contempt; but a truly noble and resolved spirit appears greatest in distress, and then becomes more bright and conspicuous. --Plutarch

Oh, how portentous is prosperity! How, comet-like, it threatens while it shines.--Young

Prosperity too often has the same effect on its possessor, that a calm at sea has on the Dutch mariner, who frequently, it is said, in these circumstances, ties up the rudder, gets drunk, and goes to sleep.--Bp. Horne

In prosperity prepare for a change; in adversity hope for one.--Burgh

To rejoice in the prosperity of another is to partake of it.--W. Austin

Many are not able to suffer and endure prosperity; it is like the light of the sun to a weak eye, glorious, indeed, in itself, but not proportioned to such an instrument.--Jeremy Taylor
There is a glare about worldly success which is very apt to dazzle men's eyes.--Hare

Greatness stands upon a precipice, and if prosperity carries a man ever so little beyond his poise, it overbears and dashes him to pieces. --Seneca

He that swells in prosperity will be sure to shrink in adversity. --Colton

Watch lest prosperity destroy generosity.--H.W. Beecher

One is never more on trial than in the moment of excessive good fortune.--Lew Wallace

The mind that is much elevated and insolent with prosperity, and cast down by adversity, is generally abject and base.--Epicurus

Nothing is harder to direct than a man in prosperity; nothing more easily managed than one in adversity.--Plutarch

PURPOSE

Thy purpose firm is equal to the deed. Who does the best his circumstance allows, does well, acts nobly; angels could no more. --Young

That man who forms a purpose which he knows to be right, and then moves forward to accomplish it without inquiring where it will land him as an individual, and without caring what the immediate consequences to himself will be, is the manliest of manly men.--John Wanamaker

It is better by a noble boldness to run the risk of being subject to half of the evils we anticipate, than to remain in cowardly listlessness for fear of what may happen.--Herodotus

It is the old lesson--a worthy purpose, patient energy for its accomplishment, a resoluteness undaunted by difficulties, and then success.--W.M. Punshon

There is no road to success but through a clear strong purpose. --Nothing can take its place.--A purpose underlies character, culture, position, attainment of every sort.--T.T. Munger

The man without a purpose is like a ship without a rudder--a waif, a nothing, a no man. Have a purpose in life, and, having it, throw such strength of mind and muscle into your work as God has given you. --Carlyle

READING

You may glean knowledge by reading, but you must separate the chaff from the wheat by thinking.

Always have a book at hand, in the parlor, on the table, for the family; a book of condensed thought and striking anecdote, of sound maxims and truthful apothegms. It will impress on your own mind a thousand valuable suggestions, and teach your children a thousand lessons of truth and duty. Such a book is a casket of jewels for your household.--Tryon Edwards

The pleasure of reading without application is a dangerous pleasure. Useless books we should lay aside, and make all possible good use of those from which we may reap some fruit.--Foster

Happy is he who has laid up in his youth, and held fast in all fortune, a genuine and passionate love for reading.--Rufus Choate

No entertainment is so cheap as reading, nor any pleasure so lasting.-
-Lady M.W. Montague

If the riches of the Indies, or the crowns of all the kingdoms of
Europe, were laid at my feet in exchange for my love of reading, I
would spurn them all.--Fenelon

The foundation of knowledge must be laid by reading. General principles must be had from books, which, however, must be brought to
the test of real life. In conversation you never get a system. What is
said upon a subject is to be gathered from a hundred people. The
parts of a truth, which a man gets thus, are at such a distance from
each other, that he never attains to a full view.--Johnson

Reading maketh a full man; conference a ready man, and writing an
exact man; and, therefore, if a man write little, he had need have a
great memory; if he confer little, he had need have a present wit; and
if he read little, he had need have much cunning, to seem to know
that he doth not.--Bacon

By reading, we enjoy the dead; by conversation, the living; and by
contemplation, ourselves. Reading enriches the memory, conversation polishes the wit; and contemplation improves the judgment. Of
these, reading is the most important, as it furnishes both the others.
--Colton

What blockheads are those wise persons, who think it necessary that
a child should comprehend everything it reads.--Southey

The love of reading enables a man to exchange the wearisome hours
of life, which come to every one, for hours of delight.--Montesquieu

Force yourself to reflect on what you read, paragraph by paragraph.
--Coleridge

Read not to contradict and confute, nor to believe and take for granted, nor to find talk and discourse, but to weigh and consider. Some
books are to be tasted, others to be swallowed, and some few to be
chewed and digested; that is, some books are to be read only in parts;
others to be read, but not curiously; and some few to be read wholly,
and with diligence and attention.--Bacon

We should be as careful of the books we read, as of the company we keep. The dead very often have more power than the living.--Tryon Edwards

He picked something valuable out of everything he read.--Pliny

No man can read with profit that which he cannot learn to read with pleasure. If I do not find in a book something which I am looking for, or am ready to receive, then the book is no book for me however much it may be for another man.--Noah Porter

Resolve to edge in a little reading every day, if it is but a single sentence.--If you gain fifteen minutes a day, it will make itself felt at the end of the year.--H. Mann

We may read, and read, and read again, and still find something new, something to please, and something to instruct.--Hardis

There are three classes of readers: some enjoy without judgment; others judge without enjoyment; and some there are who judge while they enjoy, and enjoy while they judge. The latter class reproduces the work of art on which it is engaged.--Its numbers are very small.--Goethe

Imprint the beauties of authors upon your imagination, and their good morals upon your heart.--C. Simmons

Every book salesman is an advance agent for culture and for better citizenship, for education and for the spread of intelligence.--Dr. Frank Crane

When I take up a book I have read before I know what to expect, and the satisfaction is not lessened by being anticipated, I shake hands with and look the old tried and valued friend in the face, compare notes, and chat the hour away.--Hazlitt

The first time I read an excellent work, it is to me just as if I had gained a new friend; and when I read over a book I have perused before, it resembles the meeting with an old one.--Goldsmith

The man who is fond of books is usually a man of lofty thought, and of elevated opinions.--Dawson

To read without reflecting, is like eating without digesting.--Burke

Insist on reading the great books, on marking the great events of the world. Then the little books can take care of themselves, and the trivial incidents of passing politics and diplomacy may perish with the using.--A.P. Stanley

Reading furnishes the mind only with materials of knowledge; it is thinking that makes what we read ours. So far as we apprehend and see the connection of ideas, so far it is ours; without that it is so much loose matter floating in our brain.--Locke

By conversing with the mighty dead we imbibe sentiment with knowledge. We become strongly attached to those who can no longer either hurt or serve us, except through the influence which they exert over the mind. We feel the presence of that power which gives immortality to human thoughts and actions, and catch the flame of enthusiasm from all nations and ages.--Hazlitt

I read for three things: first, to know what the world has done during the last twenty-four hours, and is about to do today; second, for the knowledge that I specially want in my work; and third, for what will bring my mind into a proper mood.--H.W. Beecher

If we encountered a man of rare intellect we should ask him what books he read.--Emerson

It was from my own early experience that I decided there was no use to which money could be applied so productive of good to boys and girls who have good within them and ability and ambition to develop it as the founding of a public library.--Andrew Carnegie

As you grow ready for it, somewhere or other, you will find what is needful for you in a book.--George MacDonald

Reading maketh a full man.--Bacon

Reading nourisheth the wit; and when it is wearied with study, it refresheth it, yet not without study.--Seneca

We are now in want of an art to teach how books are to be read rather than to read them. Such an art is practicable.--Disraeli

Read, mark, learn, and inwardly digest.--Collect

Learn to read slow; all other graces will follow in their proper places.
--W. Walker

He that I am reading seems always to have the most force.
--Montaigne

Reading Chaucer is like brushing through the dewy grass at sunrise.
--Lowell

We should accustom the mind to keep the best company by intro-
ducing it only to the best books.--Sydney Smith

We have not read an author till we have seen his object, whatever it
may be, as he saw it.--Carlyle

He found shelter among books, which insult not, and studies that ask
no questions of a youth's finances.--Lamb

'Tis the good reader that makes the good book; a good head cannot
read amiss, in every book he finds passages which seem confidences
or asides hidden from all else and unmistakably meant for his ear.
--Emerson

The man whose bosom neither riches nor luxury nor grandeur can
render happy may, with a book in his hand, forget all his dorments
under the friendly shade of every tree; and experience pleasures as
infinite as they are varied, as pure as they are lasting, as lively as they
are unfading, and as compatible with every public duty as they are
contributory to private happiness.--Zimmermann

My early and invincible love of reading,*** I would not exchange for
the treasures of India.--Gibbon

A good reader is nearly as rare as a good writer. People bring their
prejudices, whether friendly or adverse. They are lamp and specta-
cles, lighting and magnifying the page.--Willmott

Men must read for amusement as well as for knowledge.--H.W.
Beecher

The way to spread a work is to sell it at a low price. No man will send to buy a thing that costs even sixpence without an intention to read it.--Johnson

Every reader reads himself out of the book that he reads; nay, has he a strong mind, reads himself into the books, and amalgamates his thoughts with the author's.--Goethe

A great work always leaves us in a state of musing.--Isaac Disraeli

People seldom read a book which is given to them; and few are given. When in reading we meet with any maxim that may be of use, we should take it for our own, and make an immediate application of it, as we would of the advice of a friend whom we have purposely consulted.--Colton

It is not the reading of many books which is necessary to make a man wise or good, but the well-reading of a few, could he be sure to have the best. And it is not possible to read over many on the same subject in great deal of loss of precious time.--Richard Baxter

Much depends upon when and where you read a book. In the five or six impatient minutes before the dinner is quite ready, who would think of taking up the Faerie Queen for a stop-gap, or a volume of Bishop Andrew's Sermons?--Lamb

I read hard, or not at all; never skimming, never turning aside to merely inviting books; and Plato, Aristotle, Butler, Thucydides, Sterne, Jonathan Edwards, have passed like the iron atoms of the blood into my mental constitution.--F.W. Robertson

I love to lose myself in other men's minds. When I am not walking, I am reading. I cannot sit and think; books think for me. I have no repugnances. Shaftesbury is not too genteel for me, nor Jonathan Wild too low.--Lamb

Books afford the surest relief in the most melancholy moments. --Zimmermann

Some read books only with a view to find fault, while others read only to be taught, the former are like venomous spiders, extracting a poisonous quality, where the latter, like the bees, sip out a sweet and profitable juice.--L'Estrange

I seek in the reading of my books only to please myself by an irreproachable diversion; or if I study it is for no other science than that which treats of the knowledge of myself, and instructs me how to die and live well.--Montaigne

There is creative reading as well as creative writing.--Emerson

Reading is to the mind what exercise is to the body. As by the one, health is preserved, strengthened, and invigorated; by the other, virtue (which is the health of the mind) is kept alive, cherished, and confirmed.--Addison

There was, it is said, a criminal in Italy who was suffered to make his choice between Guicciardini and the galleys. He chose the history. But the war of Pisa was too much for him; he changed his mind, and went to the oars.--Macaulay

When I am reading a book, whether wise or silly, it seems to me to be alive and talking to me.--Swift

Reading without purpose is sauntering, not exercise. More is got from one book on which the thought settles for a definite end in knowledge, than from libraries skimmed over by a wandering eye. A cottage flower gives honey to the bee, and king's garden none to the butterfly.--Bulwer-Lytton

A man who has any relish for fine writing either discovers new beauties or receives stronger impressions from the masterly strokes of a great author every time he peruses him; besides that he naturally wears himself into the same manner of speaking and thinking. --Addison

If thou wilt receive profit, read with humility, simplicity, and faith; and seek not at any time the fame of being learned.--Thomas a Kempis

Learn to be good readers, which is perhaps a more difficult thing than you imagine. Learn to be discriminative in your reading; to read faithfully, and with your best attention, all kinds of things which you have a real interest in,--a real, not an imaginary,--and which you find to be really fit for what you are engaged in.--Carlyle

The habit of reading is the only enjoyment I know in which there is no alloy. It lasts when all other pleasures fade. It will be there to support you when all other resources are gone. It will be present to you when the energies of your body have fallen away from you. It will last you until your death. It will make your hours pleasant to you as long as you live.--Trollope

There is a world of science necessary in choosing books. I have known some people in great sorrow fly to a novel, or the last light book in fashion. One might as well take a rose-draught for the plague! Light reading does not do when the heart is really heavy. I am told that Goethe, when he lost his son, took to study a science that was new to him. Ah! Goethe was a physician who knew what he was about.--Bulwer-Lytton

By conversing with the mighty dead, we imbibe sentiment with knowledge. We become strongly attached to those who can no longer either hurt or serve us, except through the influence which they exert over the mind. We feel the presence of that power which gives immortality to human thoughts and actions, and catch the flame of enthusiasm from all nations and ages.--Hazlitt

Have you ever rightly considered what the mere ability to read means? That it is the key which admits us to the whole world of thought and fancy and imagination? To the company of saint and sage, of the wisest and the wittiest at their wisest and wittiest moment? That it enables us to see with the keenest eyes, hear with the finest ears, and listen to the sweetest voices of all time! More than that, it annihilates time and space for us.--Lowell

He that loves reading has everything within his reach. He has but to desire, and he may possess himself of every species of wisdom to judge and power to perform.--William Godwin

They that have read about everything are thought to understand everything too; but it is not always so. Reading furnishes the mind only with the materials of knowledge; it is thinking that makes what we read ours. We are of the rumination kind, and it is not enough to cram ourselves with a great load of collections,--we must chew them over again.--Channing

The first class of readers may be compared to an hour-glass, their reading being as the sand; it runs in and runs out, and leaves not a vestige behind. A second class resembles a sponge, which imbibes everything, and returns it in nearly the same state, only a little dirtier. A third class is like a jellybag, which allows all that is pure to pass away, and retains only the refuse and dregs. The fourth class may be compared to the slave of Golconda, who, casting aside all that is worthless, preserves only the pure gems.--Coleridge

RELIGION

Religion, so far as it is genuine, is in essence the response of created personalities to the Creating Personality, God. "This is life eternal, that they might know thee the only true God, and Jesus Christ, whom thou hast sent."--A.B. Tozer

Indisputably the believers in the gospel have a great advantage over all others, for this simple reason, that, if true, they will have their reward hereafter; and if there be no hereafter, they can but be with the infidel in his eternal sleep, having had the assistance of an exalted hope through life, without subsequent disappointment.--Byron

Depend upon it religion is, in its essence, the most gentlemanly thing in the world. It will alone gentilize, if unmixed with cant; and I know nothing else that will, alone.--Coleridge

True religion is the foundation of society, the basis on which all true civil government rests, and from which power derives its authority, laws their efficacy, and both their sanction. If it is once shaken by contempt, the whole fabric cannot be stable or lasting.--Burke

Should a man happen to err in supposing the Christian religion to be true, he could not be a loser by the mistake. But how irreparable is his loss, and how inexpressible his danger, who should err in supposing it to be false.--Pascal

As to Jesus of Nazareth, my opinion of whom you particularly desire, I think the system of morals and His religion, as He left them to us, is the best the world ever saw, or is likely to see.--Franklin

Religion cannot pass away. The burning of a little straw may hide the stars of the sky, but the stars are there, and will reappear.--Carlyle

The task and triumph of religion is to make men and nations true and just and upright in all their dealings, and to bring all law as well as all conduct into subjection and conformity to the law of God.--H.J. Van Dyke

Religion is the first thing and the last thing, and until a man has found God and been found by God, he begins at no beginning, he works to no end.--H.G. Wells

Religion does what philosophy could never do.--It shows the equal dealings of heaven to the happy and the unhappy, and levels all human enjoyments to nearly the same standard.--It offers to both rich and poor the same happiness hereafter, and equal hopes to aspire after it.--Goldsmith

Of all the dispositions and habits which lead to political prosperity, religion and morality are indispensable supporters.--A volume could not trace all their connections with private and public felicity. --Washington

The writers against religion, while they oppose every system, are wisely careful never to set up any of their own.--Burke

Religion is the best armor in the world, but the worst cloak.--John Newton

While men believe in the possibilities of children being religious, they are largely failing to make them so, because they are offering them not a child's but a man's religion--men's forms of truth and men's forms of experience.--Phillip Brooks

When I was young, I was sure of many things; now there are only two things of which I am sure: one is, that I am a miserable sinner; and the other, that Jesus Christ is an all-sufficient Saviour.--He is well taught who learns these two lessons.--John Newton

If men are so wicked with religion, what would they be without it! --Franklin

What I want is, not to possess religion, but to have a religion that shall possess me.--Charles Kingsley

Unless we place our religion and our treasure in the same thing religion will always be sacrificed.--Epictetus

There are those to whom a sense of religion has come in storm and tempest; there are those whom it has summoned amid scenes of revelry and idle vanity; there are those, too, who have heard its "still small voice" amid rural leisure and placid retirement. But perhaps the knowledge which causeth not to err is most frequently impressed upon the mind during the season of affliction.--Walter Scott

True religion teaches us to reverence what is under us, to recognize humility; poverty, wretchedness, suffering, and death, as things divine.--Goethe

The main object of the gospel is to establish two principles,--the corruption of nature, and the redemption by Christ Jesus.--Pascal

The bible represents religion, not as the latest fruit of life, but as the whole of it--beginning, middle, and end; it is simply right living. --H.W. Beecher

Religion is the fear and love of God; its demonstration is good works; and faith is the root of both, for without faith we cannot please God; nor can we fear and love what we do not believe.--Penn

I have taken much pains to know everything that is esteemed worth knowing amongst men; but with all my reading, nothing now remains to comfort me at the close of this life but this passage of St. Paul: "It is a faithful saying, and worthy of all acceptation, that Jesus Christ came into the world to save sinners." To this I cleave, and herein do I find rest.--Seldon

If we are told a man is religious, we still ask, 'What are his morals?' But if we hear at first that he has honest morals, and is a man of natural justice and good temper, we seldom think of the other question, whether he be religious and devout.--Shaftesbury

A man's religion is himself. If he is right-minded toward God, he is religious; if the Lord Jesus Christ is his school-master, then he is Christianly religious.--H.W. Beecher

Religion is life essential.--George MacDonald

I have now disposed of all my property to my family.--There is one thing more I wish I could give them, and that is the Christian religion.--If they had that, and I had not given them one shilling, they would have been rich, and if they had not that, and I had given them all the world, they would be poor.--Patrick Henry

Leave the matter of religion to the family altar, the church, and the private school, supported entirely by private contributions; keep the Church and the State forever apart.--U.S. Grant

If there be not a religious element in the relations of men, such relations are miserable and doomed to ruin.--Carlyle

The ship retains her anchorage, yet drifts with a certain range, subject to wind and tide; so we have for an anchorage the cardinal truths of the gospel.--Gladstone

A man with no sense of religious duty is he whom the Scriptures describe in such terse but terrific language, as living "without God in the world." Such a man is out of his proper being, out of the circle of all his duties, out of the circle of all his happiness, and away, far, far away, from the purposes of his creation.--Webster

In vain do science and philosophy pose as the arbiters of the human mind, of which they are in fact only the servants. Religion has provided a conception of life, and science travels in the beaten path. Religion reveals the meaning of life, and science only applies this meaning to the course of circumstances.--Tolstoi

If we traverse the world, it is possible to find cities without walls, without letters, without kings, without wealth, without coin, without schools and theaters; but a city without a temple, or that practiceth not worship, prayer, and the like, no one ever saw.--Plutarch

Religion--that voice of the deepest human experience.--Matthew Arnold

Let us with caution indulge the supposition that morality can be maintained without religion. Reason and experience both forbid us to hope that national morality can prevail in the exclusion of religious principles.--Washington

The command of one's self is the greatest empire a man can aspire unto, and consequently, to be subject to our own passions is the most grievous slavery. He who best governs himself is best fitted to govern others.

Conquer thyself. Till thou hast done this, thou art but a slave; for it is almost as well to be subjected to another's appetite as to thine own.--Burton

He who reigns within himself and rules his passions, desires and fears is more than a king.--Milton

The man who Heaven appoints to govern others, should himself first learn to bend his passions to the sway of reason.--Thomson

For want of self-restraint many men are engaged all their lives in fighting with difficulties of their own making, and rendering success impossible by their own cross-grained ungentleness; whilst others, it may be much less gifted, make their way and achieve success by simple patience, equanimity, and self-control.--Smiles

Every temptation that is resisted, every noble aspiration that is encouraged, every sinful thought that is repressed, every bitter word that is withheld, adds its little item to the impetus of that great movement which is bearing humanity onward toward a richer life and higher character.--Fiske

What is the best government?--That which teaches us to govern ourselves.--Goethe

To rule self and subdue our passions is the more praiseworthy because so few know how to do it.--Guiana

More dear in the sight of God and His angels than any other conquest is the conquest of self.--A.P. Stanley

Let not any one say that he cannot govern his passions, nor hinder them from breaking out and carrying him to action; for what he can do before a prince or a great man, he can do alone, or in the presence of God if he will.--Locke

He that lays down precepts for governing our lives and moderating our passions, obliges humanity not only in the present, but for all future generations.--Seneca

Those who can command themselves, command others.--Hazlitt

I will have a care of being a slave to myself, for it is a perpetual, a shameful, and the heaviest of all servitudes; and this may be done by uncontrolled desires.--Seneca

One of the most important, but one of the most difficult things for a powerful mind is, to be its own master. A pond may lie quiet in a plain; but a lake wants mountains to compass and hold it in. --Addison

A man must first govern himself, ere he be fit to govern a family; and his family, ere he be fit to bear the government in the common-wealth.--Sir W. Raleigh

No conflict is so severe as his who labors to subdue himself.--Thomas a Kempis

Real glory springs from the silent conquest of ourselves; without that the conqueror is only the first slave.--Thomson

Do you want to know the man against whom you have most reason to guard yourself? Your looking-glass will give you a very fair likeness of his face.--Whately

Over the times thou has no power.--To redeem a world sunk in dishonesty has not been given thee. Solely over one man therein thou hast a quite absolute, uncontrollable power.--Him redeem and make honest.--Carlyle

It is the man who is cool and collected, who is master of his countenance, his voice, his actions, his gestures, of every part, who can work upon others at his pleasure.--Diderot

No man is free who cannot command himself.--Pythagoras

Wouldst thou have thy flesh obey thy spirit? Then let thy spirit obey thy God. Thou must be governed, that thou may'st govern. --Augustine

No one who cannot master himself is worthy to rule, and only he can rule.--Goethe

May I govern my passions with absolute sway, and grow wiser and better as life wears away.--Watts

Most powerful is he who has himself in his own power.--Seneca

SELF-KNOWLEDGE

Go to your bosom, knock there, and ask your heart what it doth know.--Shakespeare

The most difficult thing in life is to know yourself.--Thales

To know thyself--in others self-concern; would'st thou know others? Read thyself--and learn!--Schiller

As long as we are flippant and stupid and shallow and think that we know ourselves, we shall never give ourselves over to Jesus Christ; but when once we become conscious that we are infinitely more than we can fathom, and infinitely greater in possibility either for good or bad than we can know, we shall be only too glad to hand ourselves over to Him--Oswald Chambers

That man must daily wiser grow, whose search is bent himself to know.--Gay

He that knows himself, knows others; and he that is ignorant of himself could not write a very profound lecture on other men's heads. --Colton

You are surprised at your imperfections,--why? I should infer from that, that your self-knowledge is small. Surely you might rather be astonished that you do not fall into more frequent and more grievous faults, and thank God for His upholding grace.--Jean Nicolas Grou

SELF-LOVE

There are different kinds of self-love. As an instinct, it is desirable and important. As a modification of true benevolence, it is commendable. But as an idolatrous affection, it is censurable.--C. Simmons

140

The greatest of all flatterers is self-love.--Rochefoucauld

Self-love is the most delicate and the most tenacious of our sentiments: a mere nothing will wound it, but nothing can kill it.

Love thyself last.--Shakespeare

The shadow of the sun is largest, when his beams are lowest. On the contrary, we are always least when we make ourselves the greatest.

In all time self-love has blinded the wisest.--Villefre

A man who loves only himself and his pleasures is vain, presumptuous, and wicked even from principle.--Vauvenargues

All other love is extinguished by self-love; beneficence, humanity, justice, and philosophy sink under it.--Epicurus

Self-love is an instrument useful but dangerous: it often wounds the hand which makes use of it, and seldom does good without doing harm.--Rousseau

Our self-love is ever ready to revolt from our better judgment, and join the enemy within.--Steele

Self-love leads men of narrow minds to measure all mankind by their own capacity.--Jane Porter

The cause of all the blunders committed by man arises from excessive self-love. For the lover is blinded by the object loved; so that he passes a wrong judgment on what is just, good and beautiful, thinking that he ought always to honor what belongs to himself in preference to truth. For he who intends to be a great man ought to love neither himself nor his own things, but only what is just, whether it happens to be done by himself or by another.--Plato

Offended self-love never forgives.--Vigee

It is falling in love with our own mistaken ideas that makes fools and beggars of half mankind.--Young

Self-love is a cup without any bottom; you might pour all the great lakes into it, and never fill it up.--O.W. Holmes

141

Would you hurt a man keenest, strike at his self-love.--Lew Wallace

The world is governed by love,--self-love.--Rivarol

Self-love was born before love.--De Finod

Self-love, as it happens to be well or ill conducted, constitutes virtue and vice.--Rochefoucauld

Self-love exaggerates our faults as well as our virtues.--Goethe

There are wounds of self-love which one does not confess to one's dearest friends.--J. Petit-Senn

Our self-love can be resigned to the sacrifice of everything but itself.
--La Harpe

O impudent! Regardful of thy own, whose thoughts are centered on thyself alone!--Dryden

Self is the great antichrist and anti-God in the world, that sets up itself above all else.--Charnock

The most amiable people are those who least wound the self-love of others.--Bruyere

That man alone loves himself rightly who procures the greatest possible good to himself through the whole of his existence, and so pursues pleasure as not to give for it more than it is worth.--Benjamin Franklin

Every man is prompted by the love of himself to imagine that he possesses some qualities superior, either in kind or degree, to those which he sees allotted to the rest of the world.--Dr. Johnson

Almost every one flatters himself that he and his are exceptionable.
--Alphonse Karr

Self-love makes as many tyrants, perhaps, as love.--Imbert

Self-love is not so vile a sin as self-neglecting.--Shakespeare

Self-love is more cunning than the most cunning man in the world. --Rouchefoucauld

Self-love is the instrument of our preservation; it resembles the provision for the perpetuity of mankind. It is necessary, it is dear to us, it gives us pleasure, and we must conceal it.--Voltaire

Every man, like Narcissus, becomes enamored of the reflection of himself, only choosing a substance instead of a shadow. His love for any particular woman is self-love at second-hand, vanity reflected, compound egotism.--Horace Smith

Oh, the incomparable contrivance of Nature, who has ordered all things in so even a method that wherever she has been less beautiful in her gifts, there she makes it up with a larger dose of self-love, which supplies the former deficits and makes all even.--Erasmus

The most notorious swindler has not assumed so many names as self-love, nor is so much ashamed of his own. She calls herself patriotism, when at the same time she is rejoicing at just as much calamity to her native country as will introduce herself into power, and expel her rivals.--Colton

It is this unquiet self-love that renders us so sensitive. The sick man, who sleeps ill, thinks the night long. We exaggerate, from cowardice, all the evils which we encounter; they are great, but our sensibility increases them. The true way to bear them is to yield ourselves up with confidence to God.--Fenelon

SIMPLICITY

Simplicity is Nature's first step, and the last of Art.--P.J. Bailey

There is a majesty in simplicity which is far above the quaintness of wit.--Pope

Simplicity, of all things, is the hardest to be copied.--Steele

In character, in manners, in style, in all things, the supreme excellence is simplicity.--Longfellow

Goodness and simplicity are indissolubly united.--The bad are the most sophisticated, all the world over, and the good the least.--H. Martineau

Nothing is more simple than greatness, indeed, to be simple is to be great.--Emerson

Purity and simplicity are the two wings with which man soars above the earth and all temporary nature.--Simplicity is in the intention; purity in the affection: Simplicity turns to God; purity unites with and enjoys him.--Thomas a Kempis

The greatest truths are the simplest; and so are the greatest men. --Hare

A childlike mind, in its simplicity, practices that science of good to which the wise may be blind.--Schiller

Upright simplicity is the deepest wisdom, and perverse craft the merest shallowness.--Barrow

SIN

Sin is not man's problem, it is God's.--Oswald Chambers

Sin is, essentially, a departure from God.--Luther

The recognition of sin is the beginning of salvation.--Luther

Sin is first pleasing, then it grows easy, then delightful, then frequent, then habitual, then confirmed, then the man is impenitent, then he is obstinate, then he is resolved never to repent, and then he is ruined. --Leighton

If thou wouldst conquer thy weakness thou must never gratify it. --No man is compelled to evil; only his consent makes it his.--It is no sin to be tempted; it is to yield and be overcome.--Penn

He who sins against men may fear discovery, but he who sins against God, is sure of it.--C.E. Jones

Use sin as it will use you; spare it not, for it will not spare you; it is your murderer, and the murderer of the world: use it, therefore, as a murderer should be used. Kill it before it kills you. You love not death; love not the cause of death.--Baxter

What is human sin but the abuse of human appetites, of human passions, of human faculties, in themselves all innocent?--R.D. Hitchcock

The deadliest sin were the consciousness of no sin.--Carlyle

Every gross act of sin is much the same thing to the conscience that a great blow is to the head; it stuns and bereaves it of all use of its senses for a time.--South

There is no sin we can be tempted to commit, but we shall find a greater satisfaction in resisting than in committing.

We are saved from nothing if we are not saved from sin. Little sins are pioneers of hell. The backslider begins with what he foolishly considers trifling with little sins. There are no little sins. There was a time when all the evil that has existed in the world was comprehended in one sinful thought of our first parent; and all the new evil is the numerous and horrid progeny of one little sin.--Howell

Whatever disunites man from God disunites man from man.--Burke

It is not only what we do, but also what we do not do, for which we are accountable.--Moliere

No sin is small.--It is against an infinite God, and may have consequences immeasurable.--No grain of sand is small in the mechanism of a watch.--J. Taylor

I could not live in peace if I put the shadow of a willful sin between myself and God.--George Eliot

Man-like it is, to fall into sin; fiend-like it is, to dwell therein; Christ-like it is, for sin to grieve; God-like it is, all sin to leave.--Longfellow

Every sin is a mistake, as well as a wrong; and the epitaph for the sinner is, "Thou fool!"--A. MacLaren

If I were sure God would pardon me, and men would not know my sin, yet I should be ashamed to sin, because of its essential baseness.--Plato

Sin is disease, deformity, and weakness.--Plato

It is not the back, but the heart, that must bleed for sin.--South

Death from sin no power can separate.--Milton

Sin is a state of mind, not an outward act.--Sewell

Sin is ashamed of sin.--Chapman

Every man has his devilish minutes.--Lavater

Every sin provokes its punishment.--A. Bronson Alcott

Few love to hear the sins they love to act.--Shakespeare

Secret sins commonly lie nearest the heart.--Thomas Brooks

Pride and conceit were the original sin of man.--Le Sage

Sin writes histories; goodness is silent.--Goethe

There is the seed of all sins--of the vilest and worst of sins--in the best of men.--Thomas Brooks

Sin is the only thing in the world which never had an infancy, that knew no minority.--South

Other men's sins are before our eyes, our own are behind our back. --Seneca

Sin may be clasped so close, we cannot see its face.--Trench

The greater part of mankind are angry with the sinner and not with the sin.--Seneca

He that avoideth not small faults, by little and little falleth into greater.--Thomas a Kempis

There is no harder work in the world than sin.--South

Sin spoils the spirit's delicacy, and unwillingness deadens its susceptibility.--Charles H. Parkhurst

The fact is that sin is the most unmanly thing in God's world. You never were made for sin and selfishness. You were made for love and obedience.--J.G. Holland

Sin is the insurrection and rebellion of the heart against God; it turns from Him, and turns against Him; it takes up arms against God. --Richard Alleine

We are all sinful. Therefore whatever we blame in another we shall find in our own bosoms.--Seneca

Confess thee freely of thy sin; for to deny each article with oath, cannot remove nor choke the strong conception that I do groan withal. --Shakespeare

O sin, what has thou done to this fair earth!--Dana

I learn the depth to which I have sunk from the length of the chain let down to up-draw me. I ascertain the mightiness of the ruin by examining the machinery for restoration.--Henry Melvill

God made sin possible just as he made all lying wonders possible, but he never made it a fact, never set anything in his plan to harmonize with it. Therefore it enters the world as a forbidden fact against everything that God has ordained.--Horace Bushnell

Never let any man imagine that he can pursue a good end by evil means, without sinning against his own soul! Any other issue is doubtful; the evil effect on himself is certain.--Southey

Sin is dark and loves the dark, still hides from itself in gloom, and in the darkest hell is still itself the darkest hell and the severest woe. --Pollok

The wicked are wicked, no doubt, and they go astray and they fall, and they come by their deserts; but who can tell the mischief which the very virtuous do?--Thackeray

The greatest penalty of evil-doing is to grow into the likeness of bad men, and, growing like them, to fly from the conversation of the good, and be cut off from them, and cleave to and follow after the company of the bad.--Plato

SUCCESS

Success covers a multitude of blunders.--H.W. Shaw

147

To think hard and quickly, see the core of a subject, seize it and base action upon it, is the secret of successfulness.--John Wanamaker

Never put your dream of success as God's purpose for you; His purpose may be exactly the opposite.--Oswald Chambers

Success we get without God doesn't count up very much.--John Wanamaker

The difference between failure and success is doing a thing nearly right and doing it exactly right.--Edward C. Simmons

Success is counted sweetest by those who ne'er succeed.--Emily Dickinson

We can do anything we want to do if we stick to it long enough. --Helen Keller

In history as in life it is success that counts. Start a political upheaval and let yourself be caught, and you will hang as a traitor. But place yourself at the head of a rebellion and gain your point and all future generations will worship you as the Father of their Country. --Hendrik Van Loon

If a man can write a better book, preach a better sermon, or make a better mousetrap than his neighbor, though he build his house in the woods, the world will make a beaten path to his door.--Generally attributed to Emerson, also claimed by Elbert Hubbard

I believe the true road to preeminent success in any line is to make yourself master of that line.--Andrew Carnegie

Possessions, outward success, publicity, luxury--to me these have always been contemptible. I believe that a simple and unassuming manner of life is best for everyone, best both for the body and the mind.--Albert Einstein

Put all good eggs in one basket and then watch that basket.--Andrew Carnegie

Success is full of promise till men get it; and then it is a last year's nest, from which the bird has flown.--Beecher

Somebody said it couldn't be done, but he with a chuckle replied that "maybe it couldn't," but he would be one who wouldn't say so til he'd tried.--Edgar A. Guest

Success consecrates the foulest crimes.--Seneca

One never learns by success. Success is the plateau that one rests upon to take breath and look down from upon the straight and difficult path, but one does not climb upon a plateau.--Josephine Preston Peabody.

A successful career has been full of blunders.--Charles Buxton

In Success be moderate.--Franklin

With the losers let it sympathize; for nothing can seem foul to those that win.--Shakespeare

The mind is hopeful; success is in God's hands. (Man proposes, God disposes.)--Plautus

Salvation is the only real success. Men are called successful who succeed in a section or two. What if three air-tight compartments keep dry, when the bulkheads break and the ship sinks? What if a man wins a boat race, a horse race, a lottery prize, and cannot speak grammatically, and does not know one good book nor one star nor tune nor flower from another, nor ever had a real friend? Is that success? Salvation is soundness. To have a splendid digestion, but a feeble mind; to have muscles standing out like whipcords, but lungs that are affected; to have perfect sight and hearing, but a weak heart, is this success? Is this soundness? Salvation is health, wholeness, holiness. It is to be right all round. I may miss perfect success in the world of business and in the world of health. I need not in the real world--the moral,--in the real life--the spiritual. God's holiness is expressed in His love. Therefore love is wholeness, and to love is to fulfill--to fill full--God's law, and be right all round. Learn then to love God and your brother and all things great and small. Life is our "chance of learning love." To make money, to win academic degrees, to lead political armies, and not to love up and down, right and left, is to have missed success. Men suspect it now. They will know it by and by.--Maltbie Babcock.

Success serves men as a pedestal. It makes them seem greater when not measured by reflection.--Joubert

The worst use that can be made of success is to boast of it.--Arthur Helps

Success has a great tendency to conceal and throw a veil over the evil deeds of men.--Demosthenes

The greatest success is confidence, or perfect understanding between sincere people.--Emerson

Success at first doth many times undo men at last.--Venning

Had I succeeded well, I had been reckoned amongst the wise; our minds are so disposed to judge from the event.--Euripides

We tell our triumphs to the crowd, but our own hearts are the sole confidants of our sorrows.--Bulwer-Lytton

Few things are impracticable in themselves; and it is for want of application rather than of means, that men fail of success. --Rochefoucauld

Better have failed in the high aim, as I, than vulgarly in the low aim succeed, as, God be thanked! I do not.--Robert Browning

I have always observed that to succeed in the world one should appear like a fool but be wise.--Montesquieu

There are but two ways of rising in the world: either by one's own industry or profiting by the foolishness of others.--La Bruyere

It is a mistake to suppose that men succeed through success; they much oftener succeed through failure.--Samuel Smiles

Success does not consist in never making blunders, but in never making the same one the second time.--H.W. Shaw

There are none so low but that they have their triumphs. Small successes suffice for small souls.--Bovee

Nothing is impossible to the man that can will. Is that necessary? That shall be. This is the only law of success.--Mirabeau

Success! to thee, as to a God, men bend the knee.--AEschylus

Whenever you see a man who is successful in society, try to discover what makes him pleasing, and if possible adopt his system. --Beaconsfield

If you wish success in life, make perseverance your bosom friend, experience your wise counselor, caution your elder brother, and hope your guardian genius.--Addison

To know a man, observe how he wins his object, rather than how he loses it; for when we fail, our pride supports us.--when we succeed, it betrays us.--Colton

The thinking part of mankind do not form their judgment from events; and their equity will ever attach equal glory to those actions which deserve success, and those which have been crowned with it. --Washington

Julius Caesar owed two millions when he risked the experiment of being general in Gaul. If Julius Caesar had not lived to cross the Rubicon, and pay off his debts, what would his creditors have called Julius Caesar?--Bulwer-Lytton

Success often costs more than it is worth.--E. Wigglesworth

He will succeed; for he believes all he says.--Mirabeau

A strenuous soul hates cheap success.--Fielding

Success makes success, as money makes money.--Chamfort

The surest way not to fail is to determine to succeed.--Sheridan

To know how to wait is the great secret of success.--De Maistre

The man who is always fortunate cannot easily have a great reverence for virtue.--Cicero

The talent of success is nothing more than doing what you can do without a thought of fame. If it comes at all it will come because it is deserved, not because it is sought after.--Longfellow

TEACHING

. . .the spheres God brings us into are not meant to teach us something but to *make* us something.--Oswald Chambers

The school is the manufactory of humanity.--Comenius

Teach the art of living well.--Seneca

Education is our only political safety.--Horace Mann

Teachers should be held in highest honor.--Mrs. Sigourney

Teach erring man to spurn the rage of gain.--Goldsmith

None can teach admirably if not loving his task.--A. Bronson Alcott

The one exclusive sign of a thorough knowledge is the power of teaching.--Aristotle

It is a luxury to learn; but the luxury of learning is not to be compared with the luxury of teaching.--Roswell D. Hitchcock

Passionate words or blows from the tutor fill the child's mind with terror and affrightment, which immediately takes it wholly up and leaves no room for other impressions.--Locke

You cannot teach a man anything; you can only help him to find it within himself.--Galileo

A teacher who is attempting to teach without inspiring the pupil with a desire to learn is hammering on cold iron.--Mann

Garden work consists much more in uprooting weeds than in planting seed. This applies also to teaching.--Auerbach

Worried and tormented into monotonous feebleness, the best part of his life ground out of him in a mill of boys.--Dickens

How shall he give kindling in whose own inward man there is no live coal, but all is burnt out to a dead grammatical cinder?--Carlyle

A teacher should, above all things, first induce a desire in the pupil for the acquisition he wishes to impart.--Mann

The authority of those who teach is very often an impediment to those who desire to learn.--Cicero

Our Lord's teaching does not mean anything to a man until it does, and then it means everything.--Oswald Chambers

The best teacher is the one who suggests rather than dogmatizes, and inspires his listener with the wish to teach himself.--Bulwer-Lytton

There is nothing more frightful than for a teacher to know only what his scholars are intended to know.--Goethe

Those who educate children well are more to be honored than they who produce them; for these only gave them life, those the art of living well.--Aristotle

Instructors should not only be skillful in those sciences which they teach, but have skill in the method of teaching, and patience in the practice.--Dr. Watts

Education of youth is not a bow for every man to shoot in that counts himself a teacher; but will require sinews almost equal to those which Homer gave to Ulysses.--Milton

In the education of children there is nothing like alluring the appetites and affection; otherwise you make so many asses laden with books.--Montaigne

There is no teaching until the pupil is brought into the same state or principle in which you are; a transfusion takes place; his is you, and you are he; there is a teaching; and by no unfriendly chance or bad company can he ever quite lose the benefit.--Emerson

Count it one of the highest virtues upon earth to educate faithfully the children of others, which so few, and scarcely any, do by their own.--Luther

Do not, then, train boys to learning by force and harshness; but direct them to it by what amuses their minds, so that you may be the better able to discover with accuracy the peculiar bent of the genius of each.--Plato

Attempt to teach the young but little at a time; this will be easier to impart, easier to receive, and surer to be retained.--Hosea Ballou

It is the duty of a man of honor to teach others the good which he has not been able to do himself because of the malignity of the times, that this good finally can be done by another more loved in heaven. --Machiavelli

It is by the promulgation of sound morals in the community, and more especially by the training and instruction of the young, that woman performs her part towards the preservation of free government.--Daniel Webster

Men want to be reminded, who do not want to be taught; because those original ideas of rectitude to which the mind is compelled to assent when they are proposed, are not always as present to us as they ought to be.--Burke

Go to the place where the thing you wish to know is native; your best teacher is there. Where the thing you wish to know is so dominant that you must breathe its very atmosphere, there teaching is most thorough, and learning is most easy. You acquire a language most readily in the country where it is spoken; you study mineralogy best among miners; and so with everything else.--Goethe

Experience teaches slowly, and at the cost of mistakes.--Froude

Our Lord is not the great Teacher of the world, He is the Saviour of the world and the Teacher of those who believe in Him, which is a radically different matter.--Oswald Chambers

TEARS

Tears are the silent language of grief.--Voltaire

More tears are shed in playhouses than in churches.--Guthrie

Tears are due to human misery.--Virgil

They that sow in tears shall reap in joy.--Bible

Those tender tears that humanize the soul.--Thomson

Tears are sometimes as weighty as words.--Ovid

Tears are the noble language of the eye.--Herrick

If you have tears, prepare to shed them now.--Shakespeare

For Beauty's tears are lovelier than her smile.--Campbell

Tears are a good alternative but a poor diet.--H.W. Shaw

Tears may soothe the wounds they cannot heal.--Thomas Paine

Every tear is a verse, and every heart is a poem.--Marc Andre

Love is loveliest when embalmed in tears.--Walter Scott

Man is the weeping animal born to govern all the rest.--Pliny

Tears soothe suffering eyes.--Richter

Scorn the proud man that is ashamed to weep.--Young

Weep for love, but not for anger; a cold rain will never bring flowers.
--Duncan

Every tear of sorrow sown by the righteous springs up a pearl.
--Matthew Henry

Let me wipe off this honorable dew, that silverly doth progress on thy
cheeks.--Shakespeare

In youth, one has tears without grief; in age, griefs without tears.
--Joseph Roux

Tears are often to be found where there is little sorrow, and the deepest sorrow without any tears.--Johnson

Lofty mountains are full of springs; great hearts are full of tears.
--Joseph Roux

I can approve of those only who seek in tears for happiness.--Pascal

Tears are nature's lotion for the eyes. The eyes see better for being washed with them.--Boves

THANKFULNESS

Giving thanks is not weakness but strength, for it involves self-repression.--Fulton Sheen

Wouldst thou first pause to thank thy God for every pleasure, for mourning over griefs thou wouldst not find the leisure.--Ruckert

Pride slays thanksgiving, but an humble mind is the soil out of which thanks naturally grows.--A proud man is seldom a grateful man, for he never thinks he gets as much as he deserves.--H.W. Beecher

If one should give me a dish of sand, and tell me there were particles of iron in it, I might look for them with my eyes, and search for them with my clumsy fingers, and be unable to detect them; but let me take a magnet and sweep through it, and how would it draw to itself the almost invisible particles by the mere power of attraction.--The unthankful heart, like my finger in the sand, discovers no mercies; but let the thankful heart sweep through the day, and as the magnet finds the iron, so it will find, in every hour, some heavenly blessings, only the iron in God's sand is gold!--H.W. Beecher

Father, we thank Thee for our food, but Lord, if we had no food, we would want to thank You just the same. Because we aren't thankful for just what You give us, we are thankful most of all for the privilege of learning to be thankful.--C.E. Jones

God's goodness hath been great to thee.--Let never day nor night unhallowed pass but still remember what the Lord hath done.
--Shakespeare

The private and personal blessings we enjoy, the blessings of immunity, safeguard, liberty, and integrity, deserve the thanksgiving of a whole life.--J. Taylor

To receive honestly is the best thanks for a good thing.--George MacDonald

Many favors which God gives us ravel out for want of hemming through our unthankfulness, for though prayer purchases blessings, giving praise keeps the quiet possession of them.--Fuller

I am glad that he thanks God for anything.--Samuel Johnson

The worship most accdptable to God, comes from a thankful and cheerful heart.--Plutarch

Our whole life should speak forth our thankfulness; every condition and place we are in should be a witness of our thankfulness. This will make the times and places we live in better for us. When we ourselves are monuments of God's mercy, it is fit we should be patterns of His praises, and leave monuments to others. We should think it given to us to do something better than to live in. We live not to live: our life is not the end of itself, but the praise of the giver.--R. Libbes

God has two dwellings: one in heaven, and the other in a meek and thankful heart.--Isaak Walton

THANKSGIVING DAY

THE FIRST PRESIDENTIAL THANKSGIVING PROCLAMATION BY THE PRESIDENT OF THE UNITED STATES OF AMERICA

A Proclamation

WHEREAS, It is the duty of all Nations to acknowledge the Providence of Almighty God, to obey his Will, to be grateful for his Benefits, and humbly to implore his Protection and Favour: And whereas both houses of Congress have, by their joint Committee, a Day of PUBLIC THANKSGIVING and PRAYER, to be observed by acknowledging with grateful Hearts the many Signal Favours of Almighty God, especially by affording them an opportunity peaceably to establish a Form of Government for their Safety and Happiness."

Now, THEREFORE, I do recommend and assign THURSDAY the Twenty-Sixth Day of November next, to be devoted by the People of these States, to the Service of that great and glorious Being, who is the beneficent Author of all the good that was, that is, or that will be: That we may then all unite in rendering unto him our sincere and humble thanks for his kind Care and Protection of the People of this Country previous to their becoming a Nation;--for the signal and manifold Mercies, and the favourable Interpositions of his Providence in the Course & Conclusion of the late War;--for the great Degree of Tranquility, Union, and Plenty, which we have since enjoyed:--for the peaceable and rational Manner in which we have been enabled to establish Constitutions of Government for our Safety and Happiness, and particularly the national one now lately instituted;--for the civil and religious Liberty with which we are blessed, and the means we have of acquiring and diffusing useful knowledge; --and in general, for all the great and various Favours which he hath been pleased to confer upon us.

AND ALSO, that we may then unite in most humbly offering our Prayers and supplications to the great Lord and Ruler of Nations, and beseech him to pardon our National and other Transgressions;--to enable us all, whether in public or private Stations, to perform our several and relative Duties properly and punctually;--to render our national Government a Blessing to all the people, by constantly being a government of wise, just and Constitutional Laws, directly and faithfully obeyed;--to protect and guide all Sovereigns and nations, (especially such as have shown kindness unto us) and to bless them with good Government, Peace and Concord;--to promote the Knowledge and Practice of true Religion and Virtue, and the increase of Science among them and us;--and generally to grant unto all mankind such a Degree of temporal Prosperity as He alone knows to be best.

Given under my Hand at the City of New York, the third Day of October, in the Year of our Lord One Thousand Seven Hundred and Eighty-Nine.--G. Washington

THOUGHT

In the end, thought rules the world. There are times when impulses and passions are more powerful, but they soon expend themselves; while mind, acting constantly, is ever ready to drive them back and work when their energy is exhausted.--J. McCosh

Great men are they who see that spiritual is stronger than any material force--that thoughts rule the world.--Emerson

Temples have their sacred images; and we see what influence they have always had over a great part of mankind; but, in truth, the ideas and images in men's minds are the invisible powers that constantly govern them; and to these they all pay universally a ready submission.--Jonathan Edwards

Nothing comes merely by thinking about it.--John Wanamaker

The key to every man is his thought. Sturdy and defying though he look, he has a helm which he obeys, which is the idea after which all his facts are classified. He can only be reformed by showing him a new idea which commands his own.--Emerson

The happiness of your life depends upon the quality of your thoughts, therefore guard accordingly; and take care that you entertain no notions unsuitable to virtue and reasonable nature.--Marcus Antoninus

A man would do well to carry a pencil in his pocket, and write down the thoughts of the moment. Those that come unsought for are commonly the most valuable, and should be secured, because they seldom return.--Bacon

Man being made a reasonable, and so a thinking creature, there is nothing more worthy of his being, than the right direction and employment of his thoughts, since upon this depend both his usefulness to the public, and his own present and future benefit in all respects.--Penn

All grand thoughts come from the heart.--Vauvengargues

Thought engenders thought. Place one idea upon paper, another will follow it, and still another, until you have written a page. You cannot fathom your mind. It is a well of thought which has no bottom. The more you draw from it, the more clear and fruitful will it be. If you neglect to think yourself, and use other people's thoughts, giving them utterance only, you will never know what you are capable of. At first your ideas may come out in lumps, homely and shapeless; but no matter; time and perseverance will arrange and polish them. Learn to think, and you will learn to write; the more you think, the better you will express your ideas.--G.A. Sala

Thinking is the talking of the soul with itself.--Plato

All truly wise thoughts have been thought already thousands of times; but to make them truly ours, we must think them over again honestly, till they take root in our personal experience.--Goethe

Our thoughts are ours, their ends none of our own.--Shakespeare

Thoughts come into our minds by avenues which are left open, and thoughts go out of our minds through avenues which we never voluntarily opened.--Emerson

A thought is often original, though you have uttered it a hundred times.--It has come to you over a new route, by a new and express train of association.--O.W. Holmes

A thinking man is the worst enemy the Prince of Darkness can have; every time such a one announces himself, I doubt not there runs a shudder through the nether empire; and new emissaries are trained with new tactics, to, if possible, entrap and hoodwink and handcuff him.--Carlyle

Second thoughts they say are best.--Dryden

160

All that a man does outwardly is but the expression and completion of his inward thought. To work effectually, he must think clearly; to act nobly, he must think nobly. Intellectual force is a principal element of the soul's life, and should be proposed by every man as the principal end of his being.--Channing

Nurture your mind with great thoughts; to believe in the heroic makes heroes.--Disraeli

The greatest events of an age are its best thoughts. It is the nature of thought to find its way into action.--Bovee

Fully to understand a grand and beautiful thought requires, perhaps, as much time as to conceive it.--Joubert

Though an inheritance of acres may be bequeathed, an inheritance of knowledge and wisdom cannot. The wealthy man may pay others for doing his work for him, but it is impossible to get his thinking done for him by another, or to purchase any kind of self-culture. --Smiles

Thoughts, even more than overt acts, reveal character.--W.S. Plumer

It is the hardest thing in the world to be a good thinker without being a good self-examiner.--Shaftesbury

Thought means life, since those who do not think do not live in any high or real sense. Thinking makes the man.--A.B. Alcott

The old thoughts never die; immortal dreams outlive their dreamers and are ours for aye; no thought once formed and uttered ever can expire.--Mackay

The men of action are, after all, only the unconscious instruments of the men of thought.--Heine

Nothing is comparable to the pleasure of an active and prevailing thought--a thought prevailing over the difficulty and obscurity of the object, and refreshing the soul with new discoveries and images of things; and thereby extending the bounds of apprehension, and as it were enlarging the territories of reason.--South

Impromptu thoughts are mental wildflowers.--Mme. du Deffand

I can readily conceive of a man without hands or feet; and I could conceive of him without a head, if experience had not taught me that by this he thinks. Thought, then, is the essence of man, and without this we cannot conceive of him.--Pascal

Before men we stand as opaque bee-hives. They can see the thoughts go in and out of us; but what work they do inside of a man they cannot tell. Before God we are as glass bee-hives, and all that our thoughts are doing within us he perfectly sees and understands. --H.W. Beecher

The only thought in the world that is worth anything is free thought. To free thought we owe all past progress and all hope for the future. Since when has anyone made it appear that shackled thought could get on better than that which is free? Brains are a great misfortune if one is never to use them.--Savage

Speech is external thought, and thought internal speech.--Rivarol

Who, with tame cowardice familiar grown, would hear my thoughts, but fear to speak their own.--Churchill

The more we examine the mechanism of thought, the more we shall see that the automatic, unconscious action of the mind enters largely into all its processes. Our definite ideas are stepping-stones; how we get from one to the other, we do not know; something carries us; we do not take the step.--Holmes

There is a thread in our thoughts, as there is a pulse in our feelings; he who can hold the one knows how to think, and he who can move the other knows how to feel.--Disraeli

The thinker requires exactly the same light as the painter, clear, without direct sunshine, or blinding reflection, and, where possible, from above.--Schlegel

Unless a man can link his written thoughts with the everlasting wants of men, so that they shall draw from them as from wells, there is no more immortality to the thoughts and feelings of the soul than to the muscles and the bones.--H.W. Beecher

Liberty of thinking, and of expressing our thoughts, is always fatal to priestly power, and to those pious frauds on which it is commonly founded.--Hume

Ingenious philosophers tell you, perhaps, that the great work of the steam engine is to create leisure for mankind. Do not believe them; it only creates a vacuum for eager thought to rush in.--George Eliot

Great thoughts, like great deeds, need no trumpet.--Bailey

Casual thoughts are sometimes of great value. One of these may prove the key to open for us a yet unknown apartment in the palace of truth, or a yet unexplored tract in the paradise of sentiment that environs it.--John Foster

Thinking is creating with God, as thinking is writing with the ready writer; and worlds are only leaves turned over in the process of composition, about his throne.--H.W. Beecher

There are few who have at once thought and capacity for action. Thought expands, but lames; action animates, but narrows.--Goethe

God put in man thought; society, action; nature, revery.--Victor Hugo

His thoughts are like mummies, embalmed in spices and wrapped about with curious envelopments; but, within, those thoughts themselves are kings.--Longfellow

Many thoughts are so dependent upon the language in which they are clothed that they would lose half their beauty of otherwise expressed.--Ruskin

If ill thoughts at any time enter into the mind of a good man, he doth not roll them under his tongue as a sweet morsel.--Matthew Henry

Whatever that be which thinks, which understands, which wills, which acts, it is something celestial and divine, and upon that account must necessarily be eternal.--Cicero

O guard thy roving thoughts with jealous care, for speech is but the dialplate of thought; and every fool reads plainly in thy words what is the our of thy thought.--Tennyson

If you are not a thinking man, to what purpose are you a man at all?
--S.T. Coleridge

Ours is the age of thought; hearts are stronger than swords.--Wendell Phillips

Mind is the great lever of all things; human thought is the process by which human ends are alternately answered.--Daniel Webster

Among mortals second thoughts are the wisest.--Euripides

Constant thought will overflow in words unconsciously.--Byron

We may divide thinkers into those who think for themselves and those who think through others; the latter are the rule, the former the exception. Only the light which we have kindled in ourselves can illuminate others.--Schopenhauer

Every thought which genius and piety throw into the world, alters the world.--Emerson

Man is but a reed, the weakest in nature, but he is a thinking reed.
--Blaise Pascal

There is no thought in any mind, but it quickly tends to convert itself into a power, and organizes a huge instrumentality of means.
--Emerson

TRIALS AND TROUBLES

The best people need afflictions for trial of their virtue. How can we exercise the grace of contentment, if all things succeed will; or that of forgiveness, if we have no enemies?--Tillotson

We are always in the forge, or on the anvil; by trials God is shaping us for higher things.--H.W. Beecher

When Anaxagoras was told of the death of his son, he only said--"I knew he was mortal." So we in all casualties of life should say, I knew my riches were uncertain; that my friend was but a man. Such considerations would soon pacify us, because all our troubles proceed from their being unexpected.--Plutarch

Trials are medicines which our gracious and wise physician prescribes, because we need them; and he proportions the frequency and weight of them to what the case requires. Let us trust in his skill, and thank him for his prescription.--J. Newton

Prosperity tries the fortunate, adversity the great.--Pliny the Younger

The hardest trial of the heart is, whether it can bear a rival's failure without triumph.--Aikin

As the musician straineth his strings, and yet he breaketh none of them but maketh thereby a sweeter melody and better concord; so God, through affliction, makes his own better unto the fruition and enjoying of the life to come.--Cawdrey

As sure as ever God puts his children in the furnace, he will be in the furnace with them.--Spurgeon

Great trials seem to be a necessary preparation for great duties. It would seem that the more important the enterprise, the more severe the trial to which the agent is subjected in his preparation. --E. Thomson

The surest way to know our gold is to look upon it and examine it in God's furnace, where he tries it that we may see what it is. If we have a mind to know whether a building stands strong or no, we must look upon it when the wind blows. If we would know whether a staff be strong, or a rotten, broken reed, we must observe it when it is leaned on and weight is borne upon it. If we would weigh ourselves justly we must weigh ourselves in God's scales that he makes use of to weigh us.--J. Edwards

Men are born to trouble at first, and are exercised in it all their days.--There is a cry at the beginning of life and a groan at the end of it. --Arnot

The little troubles and worries of life, so many of which we meet, may be as stumbling blocks in our way, or we may make them stepping-stones to a noble character and to Heaven.

Troubles are often the tools by which God fashions us for better things.--H.W. Beecher

Great faith must have great trials.--Spurgeon

If you tell your troubles to God, you put them into the grave; they will never rise again when you have committed them to him. If you roll your burden anywhere else, it will roll back again, like the stone of Sisyphus.--Spurgeon

Trouble is the next best thing to enjoyment; there is no fate in the world so horrible as to have no share in either its joys or sorrows. --Longfellow

Set about doing good to somebody. Put on your hat, and go and visit the sick and poor of your neighborhood; inquire into their circumstances, and minister to their wants. Seek out the desolate, and afflicted, and oppressed, and tell them of the consolations of religion. I have often tried this method, and have always found it the best medicine for a heavy heart.--Howard

There are many troubles which you cannot cure by the Bible and the hymn book, but which you can cure by a good perspiration and a breath of fresh air.--H.W. Beecher

The true way of softening one's troubles is to solace those of others. --Mad. De Maintenon

In all troublous events we may find comfort, though it be only in the negative admission that things might have been worse.--Barr

Trials teach us what we are.--Spurgeon

When He hath tried me, I shall come forth as gold.--Bible

Rocks whereon greatest men have oftest wreck'd.--Milton

By His trials, God means to purify us, to take away all our self-confidence, and our trust in each other, and bring us into implicit, humble trust in Himself.--Horace Bushnell

"Tribulation worketh patience; and patience, experience; and experience, hope." That is the order. You cannot put patience and experience into a parenthesis, and, omitting them, bring hope out of tribulation.--Alexander Maclaren

There will be no Christian but will have a Gethsemane; but every praying Christian will find that there is no Gethsemane without its angel!--T. Binney

Trifling troubles find utterance; deeply felt pangs are silent.--Seneca

Jesus wept once; possibly more than once. There are times when God asks nothing of His children except silence, patience, and tears. --Charles S. Robinson

When our troubles are many we are often by grace made courageous in serving our God; we feel that we have nothing to live for in this world, and we are driven, by hope of the world to come, to exhibit zeal, self-denial, and industry.--C.H. Spurgeon

It is not designed that the road should be made too smooth for us here upon earth.--Jane Porter

Never was there a man of deep piety, who has not been brought into extremities--who has not been put into fire--who has been taught to say, "Though He slay me, yet will I trust in Him."--Richard Cecil

God has not chosen to save us without crosses; as He has not seen fit to create men at once in the full vigor of manhood, but has suffered them to grow up by degrees amid all the perils and weaknesses of youth.--Fenelon

It is the easiest thing in the world for us to obey God when He commands us to do what we like, and to trust Him when the path is all sunshine. The real victory of faith is to trust God in the dark, and through the dark. Let us be assured of this, that if the lesson and the rod are of His appointing, and that His all-wise love has engineered the deep tunnel of trial on the heavenward road, He will never desert us during the discipline. The vital thing for us is not to deny and desert Him.--T.L. Cuyler

Troubles, like babies, grow large by nursing.--Lady Holland

The true way to soften one's troubles is to solace those of others. --Mme. de Maintenon

No evil lost is wailed when it is gone.--Shakespeare

Trouble and perplexity drive us to prayer, and prayer driveth away trouble and perplexity.--Melancthon

The greater our dread of crosses, the more necessary they are for us. --Fenelon

Man is born to trouble, as the sparks fly upward.--Bible

In this wild world the fondest and the best are the most tried, most troubled and distressed.--Crabbe

Know this, that troubles come swifter than the things we desire. --Plautus

There are people who are always anticipating trouble, and in this way they manage to enjoy many sorrows that never really happen to them.--H.W. Shaw

Crosses are of no use to us but inasmuch as we yield ourselves up to them and forget ourselves.--Fenelon

Troubles are exceedingly gregarious in their nature, and flying in flocks are apt to perch capriciously.--Dickens

Are you borne down by trouble, remember the apt words of Carlyle: "The eternal stars shine out as soon as it is dark enough."--H.W. Beecher

Tribulation will not hurt you unless it does--what, alas! it too often does--unless it hardens you, and makes you sour and narrow and skeptical.--Chapin

Let a man who wants to find abundance of employment procure a woman and a ship; for no two things do produce more trouble if you begin to equip them; neither are these two things ever equipped enough.--Plautus

I saw a delicate flower had grown up two feet high between the horse's path and the wheel track. An inch more to the right or left had sealed its fate, or an inch higher; and yet it lived to flourish as much as if it had a thousand acres of untrodden space around it, and never knew the danger it incurred. It did not borrow trouble, nor invite an evil fate by apprehending it.--Thoreau

Make up your mind to the prospect of sustaining a certain measure of pain and trouble in your passage through life. By the blessing of God this will prepare you for it; it will make you thoughtful and resigned without interfering with your cheerfulness.--J.H. Newman

TIME

As every thread of gold is valuable, so is every moment of time. --J. Mason

The great rule of moral conduct is, next to God, to respect time. --Lavater

The race is not to the swift, nor the battle to the strong, neither yet bread to the wise, nor yet riches to men of understanding, nor yet favor to men of skill, but time and chance happeneth to them all. --Elbert Hubbard

If time be of all things the most precious, wasting time must be the greatest produgality, since lost time is never found again; and what we call time enough always proves little enough. Let us then up and be doing, and doing to the purpose; so by diligence shall we do more with less perplexity.--Franklin

We always have time enough, if we will but use it aright.--Goethe

Spend your time in nothing which you know must be repented of; in nothing on which you might not pray for the blessing of God; in nothing which you could not review with a quiet conscience on your dying bed; in nothing which you might not safely and properly be found doing if death should surprise you in the act.--Baxter

Time will discover everything to posterity; it is a babbler, and speaks even when no question is put.--Euripides

You'll find as you grow older that you weren't born such a very great while ago after all. The time shortens up.--William Dean Howells

Time is so fleeting that if we do not remember God in our youth, age may find us incapable of thinking about Him.--Hans Christian Andersen

Measure, time and number are nothing but modes of thought or rather of imagination.--Benedict Spinoza

The end crowns all; and that old common arbitrator, time, will one day end it.--Shakespeare

The same object seen from the three different points of view--the past, the present, and the future--often exhibits three different faces to us; like those sign-boards over shop doors, which represent the face of a lion as we approach, of a man when we are in front, and of an ass when we have passed.--Longfellow

New time always! Old time we cannot keep. Time does not become sacred to us until we have lived it, until it has passed over us and taken with it a part of ourselves.--John Burroughs

It is better to be doing the most insignificant thing than to reckon even a half-hour insignificant.--Goethe

A man that is young in years may be old in hours, if he has lost no time.--Bacon

I wasted time, and now doth time waste me.--Shakespeare

Lost wealth may be replaced by industry, lost knowledge by study, lost health by temperance or medicine, but lost time is gone forever. --Smiles

What is time?--The shadow on the dial, the striking of the clock, the running of the sand, day and night, summer and winter, months, years, centuries--these are but the arbitrary and outward signs--the measure of time, not time itself. Time is the life of the soul. --Longfellow

There is not a single moment in life that we can afford to lose. --Goulburn

Dost thou love life? Then do not squander time, for that is the stuff life is made of.--Franklin

Know the true value of time; snatch, seize, and enjoy every moment of it.--No idleness; no laziness; no procrastination;--never put off till tomorrow what you can do today.--Chesterfield

The greatest loss of time is delay and expectation, which depend upon the future. We let go the present, which we have in our power, and look forward to that which depends upon chance,--and so relinquish a certainty for an uncertainty.--Seneca

A man's time, when well husbanded, is like a cultivated field, of which a few acres produces more of what is useful to life, than extensive provinces, even of the richest soil, when overrun with weeds and brambles.--Hume

Well arranged time is the surest mark of a well arranged mind. --Pitman

TRUTH

Truth is a glorious but hard mistress. She never consults, bargains or compromises.--A.W. Tozer

The worst kind of lying is making promises that you cannot fulfill. --J. Wanamaker

Christianity knows no truth which is not the child of love and the parent of duty.--Phillips Brooks

Truth, whether in or out of fashion, is the measure of knowledge, and the business of the understanding; whatsoever is beside that, however authorized by consent, or recommended by rarity, is nothing but ignorance, or something worse.--Locke

Truth is the foundation of all knowledge and the cement of all societies.--Dryden

Truth, whether in or out of fashion, is the measure of knowledge, and the business of the understanding; whatsoever is beside that, however authorized by consent, or recommended by rarity, is nothing but ignorance, or something worse.--Locke

It is easier to perceive error than to find truth, for the former lies on the surface and is easily seen, while the latter lies in the depth, where few are willing to search for it.--Goethe

Statistics-I can prove anything by statistics-except the truth.--G. Canning

What we have in us of the image of God is the love of truth and justice.--Demosthenes

General, abstract truth is the most precious of all blessings; without it man is blind, it is the eye of reason.--Rousseau

Truth lies in character. Christ did not simply speak the truth; he was truth. Truth is a thing not of words, but of life and being.--Robertson

The deepest truths are the simplest and the most common.--F.W. Robertson

Unused truth becomes as useless as an unused muscle.--A.B. Tozer

If a thousand old beliefs were ruined in our march to truth we must still march on.--Stopford A. Brooke

You need not tell all the truth, unless to those who have a right to know it all. But let all you tell be truth.--Mann

One of the sublimest things in the world is plain truth.--Bulwer

A truth that is merely acquired from others only clings to us as a limb added to the body, or as a false tooth, or a wax nose. A truth we have acquired by our own mental exertions, is like our natural limbs, which really belong to us.--This is exactly the difference between an original thinker and the mere learned man.--Schopenhauer

Truth is not only violated by falsehood; it may be equally outraged by silence.--Amien

Fear is not in the habit of speaking truth; when perfect sincerity is expected, perfect freedom must be allowed; nor has anyone who is apt to be angry when he hears the truth, any cause to wonder that he does not hear it.--Tacitus

I believe that it is better to tell the truth than a lie. I believe it is better to be free than to be a slave. And I believe it is better to know than be ignorant.--H.L Mencken

No truth so sublime but it may be seen to be trivial tomorrow in the light of new thoughts.--Emerson

Without seeking, truth cannot be known at all. It can neither be declared from pulpits, nor set down in articles, nor in any wise prepared and sold in packages ready for use. Truth must be found for every man by himself out of its husk with such help as he can get, indeed, but not without stern labor of his own.--Ruskin

There are two peculiarities in the truths of religion: a divine beauty which renders them lovely, and a holy majesty which makes them venerable.--And there are two peculiarities in errors: an impiety which renders them horrible, and an impertinence which renders them ridiculous.--Pascal

"There is nothing," says Plato, "so delightful as the hearing or the speaking of truth."--for this reason there is no conversation so agreeable as that of the man of integrity, who hears without any intention to betray, and speaks without any intention to deceive.--Sherlock

Truth is always consistent with itself, and needs nothing to help it out; it is always near at hand and sits upon our lips, and is ready to drop out before we are aware; whereas a lie is troublesome, and sets a man's invention on the rack, and one trick needs a great many more of the same kind to make it good.--Tillotson

When a man has no design but to speak plain truth, he may say a great deal in a very narrow compass.--Steele

Honesty of thought and speech and written word is a jewel, and they who curb prejudice and seek honorably to know and speak the truth are the only builders of a better life.--John Galsworthy

A truth that disheartens because it is true is of far more value than the most stimulating of falsehoods.--Maeterlinck

The old faiths light their candles all about, but burly Truth comes by and blows them out.--Lizette Woodworth Reese

Perfect truth is possible only with knowledge, and in knowledge the whole essence of the thing operates on the soul and is joined essentially to it.--Spinoza

Ultimately, our troubles are due to dogma and deduction; we find no new truth because we take some venerable but questionable proposition as the indubitable starting point, and never think of putting this assumption itself to a test of observation or experiment.--W. Durant

It is strange but true; for truth is always strange, stranger than fiction.--Byron

Funny how people despise platitudes, when they are usually the truest thing going. A thing has to be pretty true before it gets to be a platitude.--Katharine Fullerton Gerould

Man with his burning soul has but an hour of breath to build a ship of truth in which his soul may sail--sail on the sea of death, for death takes toll of beauty, courage, youth, of all but truth.--John Masefield

Scientific truth is marvellous, but moral truth is divine; and whoever breathes its air and walks by its light has found the lost paradise. --Horace Mann

Truth will never be tedious unto him that travelleth in the secrets of nature; there is nothing but falsehood that glutteth us.--Seneca

A truth which one has never heard causes the soul surprise at first, which touches it keenly; but when it is accustomed to it, becomes very insensible there.--Nicole

Truth is a naked and open daylight, that doth not show the masks and mummeries of the world half so stately and daintily as candlelights.--Bacon

But God Himself is truth; in propagating which, as men display a greater integrity and zeal, they approach nearer to the similitude of God, and possess a greater portion of his love.--Milton

The best way to come to truth being to examine things as really they are, and not to conclude they are, as we fancy of ourselves, or have been taught by others to imagine.--Locke

Truth is a thing immortal and perpetual, and it gives to us a beauty that fades not away in time, nor does it take away the freedom of speech which proceeds from justice; but it gives to us the knowledge of what is just and lawful, separating from them the unjust and refuting them.--Epictetus

Truth is tough. It will not break, like a bubble, at a touch; nay, you may kick it about all day, like a football, and it will be round and full at evening.--O.W. Holmes

Truth is the source of every good to gods and men. He who expects to be blessed and fortunate in this world should be a partaker of it from the earliest moment of his life.--Plato

Oh how great is the power of truth! which of its own power can easily defend itself against all the ingenuity and cunning and wisdom of men, and against the treacherous plots of all the world.--Cicero

Truth is a very different thing from fact; it is the loving contact of the soul with spiritual fact, vital and potent. It does not work in the soul independently of all faculty or qualification there for setting it forth or defending it. Truth in the inward parts is a power, not an opinion. --George MacDonald

There is an inward state of the heart which makes truth credible the moment it is stated. It is credible to some men because of what they are. Love is credible to a loving heart; purity is credible to a pure mind; life is credible to a spirit in which life beats strongly--it is incredible to other men.--F.W. Robertson

The greatest truths are wronged if not linked with beauty, and they win their way most surely and deeply into the soul, when arranged in this their natural and fit attire.--Channing

Truth travels down from the heights of philosophy to the humblest walks of life, and up from the simplest perceptions of an awakened intellect to the discoveries which almost change the face of the world. At every state of its progress it is genial, luminous, creative.--Everett

There is something very sublime, though very fanciful, in Plato's description of the Supreme Being,--that truth is His body and light His shadow. According to this definition there is nothing so contradictory to his nature as error and falsehood.--Addison

The dictum that truth always triumphs over persecution is one of those pleasant falsehoods which men repeat after one another till they pass into common places, but which all experience refutes.--J. Stuart Mill

Every newly discovered truth judges the world, separates the good from the evil, and calls on faithful souls to make sure of their election.--Julia Ward Howe

Ye shall know the truth and the truth shall make you free.--Anon.

Truth is the beginning of every good thing, both in heaven and on earth; and he who would be blessed and happy should be from the first a partaker of the truth, that he may live a true man as long as possible, for then he can be trusted; but he is not to be trusted who loves voluntary falsehood, and he who loves involuntary falsehood is a fool.--Plato

I am the way the truth and the life. No man cometh unto the Father but by me.--Jesus Christ

UNDERSTANDING

Humility is the light of the understanding.--Bunyan

The light of the understanding, humility and humanity kindleth and pride covereth.--Quarles

The power of perception is that which we call the understanding. --Locke

Women have the understanding of the heart, which is better than that of the head.--Rogers

It is by no means necessary to understand things to speak confident-ly about them.--Beaumarchais

Whatever we well understand we express clearly, and words flow with ease.--Boileau

I know no evil so great as the abuse of the understanding, and yet there is no one vice more common.--Steele

It is the same with understanding as with eyes: to a certain size and make, just so much light is necessary, and no more. Whatever is beyond brings darkness and confusion.--Shaftesbury

Knowing is seeing. ***Until we ourselves see it with our own eyes, and perceive it by our own understandings, we are as much in the dark and as void of knowledge as before, let us believe any learned author as much as we will.--John Locke

It is the understanding that sees and hears; it is the understanding that improves everything, that orders everything, and that acts, rules, and reigns.--Epicharmus

Fully to understand a grand and beautiful thought requires, perhaps, as much time as to conceive it.--Joubert

The improvement of the understanding is for two ends: first, our own increase of knowledge; secondly, to enable us to deliver and make out that knowledge to others.--Locke

What we do not understand we do not possess.--Goethe

A distinction has been made between acuteness and subtlety of understanding. This might be illustrated by saying that acuteness consists in taking up the points or solid atoms, subtlety in feeling the air of truth.--Hazlitt

He who calls in the aid of any equal understanding, doubles his own; and he who profits of a superior understanding, raises his powers to a level with the height of the superior understanding he unites with. --Burke

The eye of the understanding is like the eye of the sense; for as you may see great objects through small crannies or holes, so you may see great axioms of nature through small and contemptible instances. --Lord Bacon

WASHINGTON

I never say anything of a man that I have the smallest scruple of saying to him.--Washington

To be prepared for war is one of the most effectual means of preserving peace.--Washington

It is our true policy to steer clear of permanent alliances with any portion of the foreign world.--Washington

When a French statesman visited this country he asked at the Continental Congress which one was George Washington. The man said, "He is the man on his knees when the Congress goes to prayer."

My brave fellows, let no sensation of satisfaction for the triumphs you have gained induce you to insult your fallen enemy. Let no shouting, no clamorous huzzaing increase their mortification. It is sufficient for us that we witness their humiliation. Posterity will huzza for us.--Washington

Labor to keep alive in your breast that little spark of celestial fire, conscience.--Washington

It is incumbent upon every person of every description to contribute to his country's welfare.--Washington

Accept of me for the merits of Thy Son Jesus Christ. I have called on Thee for pardon and forgiveness of sins, but so coldly and carelessly, that my prayers are become my sin and stand in need of pardon. I have heard Thy holy Word, but with such deadness of spirit that I have been an unprofitable and forgetful hearer. Cover my sins with that absolute obedience of Thy dear Son that those sacrifices which I have offered may be acceptable by it to Thee, in and for the sake of the sacrifice of Jesus Christ, offered upon the cross for me. Direct my thoughts, words and work. Wash away my sins in the immaculate blood of the Lamb. And purge my heart by Thy Holy Spirit from the dross of my natural corruption. Increase my faith in the sweet promises of the Gospel. Thou gavest Thy Son to die for me. --Washington

Against the insidious wiles of foreign influence the jealousy of a free people ought to be constantly awake.--Washington

Let us impart all the blessings we possess, or ask for ourselves, to the whole family of mankind.--Washington

There can be no greater error than to expect or calculate upon real favors from nation to nation.--Washington

Every attempt to alienate any portion of our country from the rest should be indignantly frowned upon.--Washington

WEALTH

Wealth can no more be created safely, and permanently held, by the mere shuffling of securities, than character can be created by shuffling cards.--J. Wanamaker

178

Wealth is not of necessity a curse, nor poverty a blessing. --Wholesome and easy abundance is better than either extreme; better for our manhood that we have enough for daily comfort; enough for culture, for hospitality, for Christian charity.--More than this may or may not be a blessing.--Certainly it can be a blessing only by being accepted as a trust.--R.D. Hitchcock

Seek not proud wealth; but such as thou mayest get justly, use soberly, distribute cheerfully, and leave contentedly, yet have not any abstract or friarly contempt of it.--Bacon

The wealth of man is the number of things which he loves and blesses, which he is loved and blessed by.--Carlyle

The way to wealth is a plain as the way to market. It depends chiefly on two words, industry and frugality; that is, waste neither time nor money, but make the best use of both. Without industry and frugality, nothing will do; and with them, everything.--Franklin

The greatest humbug in the world is the idea that money can make a man happy. I never had any satisfaction with mine until I began to do good with it.--C. Pratt

Gold is worse poison to men's souls, doing more murders in this loathsome world, than any mortal drug.--Shakespeare

He is richest who is content with the least, for content is the wealth of nature.--Socrates

There is no security against the perils of wealth except in becoming rich toward God.--C. Simmons

If you would take your possessions into the life to come, convert them into good deeds.--Anon.

He that will not permit his wealth to do any good to others while he is living, prevents it from doing any good to himself when he is dead; and by an egotism that is suicidal and has a double edge, cuts himself off from the truest pleasure here and the highest happiness hereafter.--Colton

The gratification of wealth is not found in mere possession or in lavish expenditure, but in its wise application.--Cervantes

Money and time are the heaviest burdens of life, and the unhappiest of all mortals are those who have more of either than they know how to use.--Johnson

If thou are rich thou are poor; for, like an ass whose back with ingots bows, thou bearest thy heavy riches but a journey, and death unloads thee.--Shakespeare

Wealth is not his that has it, but his that enjoys it.--Franklin

The secret of making money is saving it. It is not what a man earns --Not the amount of his income, but the relation of his expenditures to his receipts, that determines his poverty or wealth.

Wealth may be an excellent thing, for it means power, leisure, and liberty.--J.R. Lowell

Riches are gotten with pain, kept with char, and lost with grief. The cares of riches lie heavier upon a good man than the inconveniences of an honest poverty.--L'Estrange

Wealth, after all, is a relative thing, since he that has little, and wants less, is richer than he that has much, and wants more.--Colton

It is only when the rich are sick that they fully feel the impotence of wealth.--Colton

The wealth of a state consists not in great treasures, solid walls, fair palaces, weapons, and armor; but its best and noblest wealth, and its truest safety, is in having learned, wise, honorable, and well-educated citizens.--Anon.

Wealth consists not in having great possessions, but in having few wants.--Epicurus

It requires a great deal of boldness and a great deal of caution to make a great fortune; and when you have got it, it requires ten times as much wit to keep it.--Rothschild

Wealth hath never given happiness, but often hastened misery; enough hath never caused misery, but often quickened happiness. --Tupper

To acquire wealth is difficult, to preserve it more difficult, but to spend it wisely most difficult of all.--E.P. Day

If thou desire to purchase honor with thy wealth, consider first how that wealth became thine; if thy labor got it, let thy wisdom keep it; if oppression found it, let repentance restore it; if thy parent left it, let thy virtues deserve it; so shall thy honor be safer, better, and cheaper.--Quarles

What a man does with his wealth depends upon his idea of happiness. Those who draw prizes in life are apt to spend tastelessly, if not viciously; not knowing that it requires as much talent to spend as to make.--E.P. Whipple

Wealth has now all the respect paid to it which is due only to virtue and to talent, but we can see what estimate God places upon it, since he often bestows it on the meanest and most unworthy of all his creatures.--Swift

Wealth has seldom been the portion and never the mark to discover good people; but God, who disposeth of all things wisely, hath denied it to many whose minds he has enriched with the greater blessings of knowledge and virtue, as the fairer testimonies of his love to mankind.--Izaak Walton

A man who possesses wealth possesses power, but it is a power to do evil as well as good.--A.S. Roe

WINE

There is a devil in every berry of the grape.--The Koran

Wine is a turncoat; first a friend, and then an enemy.--Fielding

O thou invisible spirit of wine, if thou hast no name to be known by, let us call thee--devil!--Shakespeare

That is a treacherous friend against whom you must always be on your guard. Such a friend is wine.--Bovee

Wine maketh the hand quivering, the eye watery, the night unquiet, lewd dreams, a stinking breath in the morning, and an utter forgetfulness of all things.--Pliny

The wine-shops breed, in physical atmosphere of malaria and a moral pestilence of envy and vengeance, the men of crime and revolution.--Charles Dickens

Wine leads to folly, making even the wise to laugh immoderately, to dance, and to utter what had better have been kept silent.--Homer

Wine makes a poor man rich in imagination, a rich man poor in reality.--Edward Parsons Day

Wine, though it possesses good qualities, was forbidden by the prophet because it attacked reason.--Hais-Bais

Wine and other luxuries have a tendency to enervate the mind and make men less brave in battle.--Caesar

Wine takes away reason, engenders insanity, leads to thousands of crimes, and imposes such an enormous expense on nations.--Pliny

Look not thou upon the wine when it is red, when it giveth its color in the cup, when it moveth itself aright: at the last it biteth like a serpent, and stingeth like an adder.--Bible

Of all things known to mortals wine is the most powerful and effectual for exciting and inflaming the passions of mankind, being common fuel to them all.--Lord Bacon

Wine intoxicates for a time, but the end is bitterness.--Lady Rachel Russell

There is never the body of a man, how strong and stout soever, if it be troubled and inflamed, but will take more harm and offense by wine being poured into it.--Plutarch

You often hear the remark that "there is no harm in a glass of wine per se". Per se means by itself. Certainly there is no harm in a glass of wine by itself. Place a glass of wine on a shelf and let it remain there, and it is per se, and will harm no own. But if you take it from the shelf and turn it inside a man, then it is no longer per se.--George W. Bain

This is the great fault in wine; it first trips up the feet, it is a cunning wrestler.--Plautus

O ye princes and rulers, how exceeding strong is wine! It causeth all men to err than drink it; it maketh the mind of the king and the beggar to be all one, of the bondman and the freeman, of the poor man and of the rich; it turneth also every thought into jollity and mirth, so that a man remembereth neither sorrow nor debt; it changeth and elevateth the spirits, and enliveneth the heavy hearts of the miserable; it maketh a man forget his brethren, and draw his sword against his best friends.--Masonic Manual

Wine is like anger; for it makes us strong, Blind and impatient; and it leads us wrong; The strength is quickly lost; we feel the error long. --Crabbe

All the crimes on earth do not destroy so much of the human race, nor alienate so much property as drunkenness.--Lord Bacon

Far from me to be the gift of Bacchus--pernicious, inflaming wine, that weakens both body and mind.--Homer of Greece

Not only has Solomon, in his wisdom, pointed out the evils, which attend those who tarry long at the wine, but all the precepts and denunciators against drunkenness, all the details of the flagitious arts penetrated under its influence, which are recorded in the Bible, from Genesis to Revelations, are directed against the inordinate drinkers of wine.--Hodgkin

Wine is the source of the greatest evils among communities. It causes diseases, quarrels, seditions, idleness, aversion to labor, and family disorders. . .It is a species of poison that causes madness. It does not make a man die, but it degrades him into a brute. Men may preserve their health and vigor without wine; with wine they run the risk of ruining their health and losing their morals.--Fenelon

Take special care that thou delight not in wine, for there never was any man who came to honor, or preferment that loved it; for it transformeth a man into a beast, decayeth health, poisoneth the breath, destroyeth natural heat, brings a man's stomach to an artificial heat, deformeth the face, rotteth the teeth, and to conclude, maketh a man contemptible, soon old, and despised of all wise and worthy men; hated in thy servants, in thyself, and companions; for it is a bewitching and infections vice.--Sir Walter Raleigh

Wine drinking is the mother of all mischief, the root of crimes, the spring of vices, the whirlwind of the brain, the overthrow of the sense, the tempest of the tongue, the ruin of the body, the shame of life, the stain of honesty, and the plague and corruption of the soul. --St. Augustine

Woe unto them that are mighty to drink wine and men of strength to mingle strong drink.--Isaiah 5:22

Light wines--nothing so treacherous. They inflame the brain like fire while melting on the palate like ice. All inhabitants of light-wine countries are quarrelsome.--Bulwer-Lytton

If it is a small sacrifice to discontinue the use of wine, do it for the sake of others; if it is a great sacrifice, do it for your own sake.--Rev. Samuel J. May

Wine heightens indifference into love, love into jealousy, and jealousy into madness. It often turns the good-natured man into an idiot, and the choleric into an assassin. It gives bitterness to resentment, it makes vanity insupportable, and displays every little spot of the soul in its utmost deformity.--Addison

WISDOM

A man can be born with ability, he can acquire knowledge, he can develop skill, but wisdom comes only from God.--Edward Hanify

Wisdom is the right use of knowledge. To know is not to be wise. Many men know a great deal, and are all the greater fools for it. There is no fool so great a fool as a knowing fool. But to know how to use knowledge is to have wisdom.--Spurgeon

Common sense in an uncommon degree is what the world calls wisdom.--Coleridge

What we call wisdom is the result of all the wisdom of past ages. --Our best institutions are like young trees growing upon the roots of the old trunks that have crumbled away.--H.W. Beecher

The Delphic oracle said I was the wisest of all the Greeks. It is because that I alone, of all the Greeks, know that I know nothing.--Socrates

The wise man is also the just, the pious, the upright, the man who walks in the way of truth. The fear of the Lord, which is the beginning of wisdom, consists in a complete devotion to God.--Zochler

Much wisdom often goes with fewest words.--Sophocles

He is wise who knows the sources of knowledge--who knows who has written and where it is to be found.--A.A. Hodge

Very few men are wise by their own counsel, or learned by their own teaching; for he that was only taught by himself had a fool to his master.--Ben Jonson

You read of but one wise man, and all that he knew was--that he knew nothing.--Congreve

True wisdom is to know what is best worth knowing, and to do what is best worth doing.--Humphreys

Wisdom is to the mind what health is to the body.--Rochefoucauld

The wise man endeavors to shine in himself; the fool to outshine others. The first is humbled by the sense of his own infirmities, the last is lifted up by the discovery of those which he observes in other men. The wise man considers what he wants, and the fool what he abounds in. The wise man is happy when he gains his own approbation, and the fool when he recommends himself to the applause of those about him.--Addison

The wisest man is generally he who thinks himself the least so. --Boileau

He that thinks himself the wisest is generally the greatest fool.-- Colton

Perfect wisdom hath four parts, vis., wisdom, the principle of doing things aright; justice, the principle of doing things equally in public and private; fortitude, the principle of not flying from danger, but meeting it; and temperance, the principle of subduing desires and living moderately.--Plato

Wisdom teaches us to do, as well as talk, and to make our words and actions all of a color.--Seneca

He is wise that is wise to himself.--Euripides

Wisdom is only found in truth.--Goethe

The two powers which in my opinion constitute a wise man are those of bearing and forbearing.--Epictetus

No one is wise at all times.--Pliny the Elder

Knowledge comes, but wisdom lingers.--Tennyson

No man is wise enough by himself.--Plautus

Body cannot teach wisdom; God only.--Emerson

Great is wisdom; infinite is the value of wisdom. It cannot be exaggerated; it is the highest achievement of man.--Carlyle

If wisdom were conferred with this proviso, that I must keep it to myself and not communicate it to others, I would have none of it. --Seneca

The first point of wisdom is to discern that which is false; the second, to know that which is true.--Lactantius

Wisdom is ofttimes nearer when we stoop than when we soar. --Wordsworth

In seeking wisdom thou art wise; in imagining that thou hast attained it thou art a fool.--Rabbi Ben-Azai

Wisdom alone is a science of other sciences and of itself.--Plato

Wisdom and eloquence are not always united.--Victor Hugo

Wisdom comes to no one by chance.--Seneca

The heart is wiser than the intellect.--J.G. Holland

Wisdom is seldom gained without suffering.--Sir Arthur Helps

He that never thinks can never be wise.--Johnson

Wisdom sits with children round her knees.--Wordsworth

For never, never wicked man was wise.--Homer

In youth and beauty wisdom is but rare!--Homer

We become wiser by adversity; prosperity destroys our appreciation of the right.--Seneca

Who then is free? The wise man who can govern himself.--Horace

The doorstep to the temple of wisdom is a knowledge of our own ignorance.--Spurgeon

It is easier to be wise for others than for ourselves. --La Rouchefoucauld

It is good to rub and polish our brain against that of others. --Montaigne

He gains wisdom in a happy way who gains it by another's experience.--Plautus

Wisdom is the talent of buying virtuous pleasures at the cheapest rate.--Fielding

A man must become wise at his own expense.--Montaigne

Look about, my son, and see how little wisdom it takes to govern the world.--Oxenstiern

He is oft the wisest man who is not wise at all.--Wordsworth

Wisdom consists not so much in seeing as in foreseeing.--Hosea Balou

Wisdom is neither gold, nor silver, nor fame, nor wealth, nor health, nor strength, nor beauty.--Plutarch

He is a wise man who does not grieve for the things which he has not, but rejoices for those which he has.--Epictetus

Wisdom consisteth not in knowing many things, nor even in knowing them thoroughly; but in choosing and in following what conduces the most certainly to our lasting happiness and true glory. --Landor

He is wise who can instruct us and assist us in the business of daily virtuous living.--Carlyle

These are the signs of a wise man: to reprove nobody, to praise nobody, to blame nobody, nor even to speak of himself or his own merits.--Epictetus

The clouds may drop down titles and estates, wealth may seek us; but wisdom must be sought.--Young

The most manifest sign of wisdom is a continual cheerfulness; her state is like that of things in the regions above the moon, always clear and serene.--Montaigne

Teach a man to read and write, and you have put into his hands the great keys of the wisdom-box.--Huxley

He who exercises wisdom exercises the knowledge which is about God.--Epictetus

Wisdom is the only thing which can relieve us from the sway of the passions and the fear of danger, and which can teach us to bear the injuries of fortune itself with moderation, and which shows us all the ways which lead to tranquility and peace.--Cicero

Wisdom is like electricity. There is no permanently wise man, but men capable of wisdom, who, being put into certain company, or other favorable conditions, become wise for a short time, as glasses rubbed acquire electric power for a while.--Emerson

Wisdom sits alone, topmost in heaven; she is its light, its God; and in the heart of man she sits as high, though groveling minds forget her oftentimes, seeing but this world's idols.--N.P. Willis

The god, O men, seems to be to be really wise; and by his oracle to mean this, that the wisdom of this world is foolishness and of none effect.--Plato

Happy is the man that findest wisdom, and the man that getteth understanding: for the merchandise of it is better than the merchandise of silver, and the gain thereof than fine gold. She is more precious than rubies: and all the things thou canst desire are not to be compared unto her. Length of days is in her right hand; and in her left hand riches and honor. Her ways are ways of pleasantness, and all her paths are peace. She is a tree of life to them that lay hold upon her; and happy is every one that retaineth her.--Bible

WORK

Work is the means of living, but it is not living.--J.G. Holland

No man's work is done on earth, so long as he can patiently labor and give anything to his family, city and nation which will add to its knowledge, wealth, improvements and importance.--John Wanamaker

The real work is putting excitement into your work.--C.E. Jones

Concentration is my motto--first honesty, then industry, then concentration.--Andrew Carnegie

When God put Adam and Eve in the garden, He did not put them there to sit and look at each other and to hold hands. He said they were to take care of the garden. You remember that--they were given something to do. Some people believe that work is a result of the curse, but that's not true. The idea is abroad that the man who works is a boob, and that work is only for fools--but God made us to work. --A.B. Tozer

Happy is the man who knows he was born to work, who knows he can work, and that by work well done he can keep on climbing as other men have done, to more enjoyable and profitable work.--John Wanamaker

Give me love and work--these two only.--William Morris

If a man love the labor of any trade, apart from any question of success or fame, the gods have called him.--Robert Louis Stevenson

A man is a worker. If he is not that, he is nothing.--Joseph Conrad

There is no truer and more abiding happiness than the knowledge that one is free to go on doing, day by day, the best work one can do, in the kind one likes best, and that this work is absorbed by a steady market and thus supports one's own life.--Perfect freedom is reserved for the man who lives by his own work and in that work does what he wants to do.--R.G. Collingwood

I never did anything worth doing by accident, nor did any of my inventions come by accident.--Thomas A. Edison

The best start for a good day's work is to be up and at it with the first hours of the morning.--John Wanamaker

I believe in work, hard work and long hours of work. Men do not break down from overwork, but from worry and dissipation. --Charles E. Hughes

We are coming to see that there should be no stifling of Labor by Capital, or of Capital by Labor; and also that there should be no stifling of Labor by Labor, or of Capital by Capital.--John D. Rockefeller, Jr.

Folks who never do any more than they get paid for, never get paid for any more than they do.--Elbert Hubbard

God didn't make things to work for us, He made us to make things work in order for Him to make us.--C.E. Jones

Learn to tell the difference between activity and work.--John Wanamaker

We have too many people who live without working, and we have altogether too many who work without living.--Dean Charles R. Brown

He who would really benefit mankind must reach them through their work.--Henry Ford

Mr. Edison says idleness is sickness: what does he know about it? He never indulged in it.--John Wanamaker

Thine to work as well as to pray.--Whittier

190

The man who does not work for the love of work but only for money is not likely to make money nor to find much fun in life.--Charles M. Schwab

Man's record upon this wild world is the record of work, and of work alone.--J.G. Holland

St. Edmund of Canterbury was right when he said to somebody, "Work as though you would live forever; but live as though you would die today."

The force, the mass of character, mind, heart or soul that a man can put into any work, is the most important factor in that work.--A.P. Peabody

I doubt if hard work, steadily and regularly carried on, ever yet hurt anybody.--Lord Stanley

Work was made for man, and not man for work. Work is man's servant, both in its results to worker and the world. Man is not work's servant, save as an almost universal perversion has made him such. --J.G. Holland

Better to wear out than to rust out.--Bishop Cumberland

Work is the inevitable condition of human life, the true source of human welfare.--Tolstoi

It is far better to give work which is above the men than to educate the men to be above their work.--Ruskin

Mind, it is our best work that He wants, not the dregs of our exhaustion. I think He must prefer quality to quantity.--George MacDonald

No work is worse than overwork; the mind preys on itself,--the most unwholesome of food.--Charles Lamb

Labor of some kind is a necessity for well-being to every human being.--John Wanamaker

The healthiest and happiest people in the world are those privileged to work a full business day.--John Wanamaker

Work is as much a necessity to man as eating and sleeping.--Even those who do nothing that can be called work still imagine they are doing something.--The world has not a man who is an idler in his own eyes.--W. Humboldt

Get work! Be sure it is better than what you work to get.--Elizabeth B. Browning

This we commanded you, that if any would not work, neither should he eat.--Bible

Unless a man works he cannot find out what he is able to do. --Hamerton

You never will be saved by works; but let us tell you most solemnly that you never will be saved without works.--T.L. Cuyler

Man must work. That is certain as the sun. But he may work grudgingly or he may work gratefully; he may work as a man, or he may work as a machine. There is no work so rude, that he may not exalt it; no work so impassive, that he may not breathe a soul into it; no work so dull that he may not enliven it.--Henry Giles

Genuine work alone, what thou workest faithfully, that is eternal as the Almighty Founder and World Builder Himself.--Carlyle

No man on earth is so happy as the man who loves his work and goes home at night with a contented heart because of a good day's work well done.--John Wanamaker

The moment a man can really do his work, he becomes speechless about it; all words are idle to him; all theories. Does a bird need to theorize about building its nest, or boast of it when built? All good work is essentially done that way; without hesitation; without difficulty; without boasting.--Ruskin

Plough deep while sluggards sleep.--Benjamin Franklin

Man hath his daily work of body or mind appointed, which declares his dignity; while other animals unactive range, and of their doings God takes no account.--Milton

We live not to ourselves, our work is life.--Bailey

No man is born into the world whose work is not born with him. There is always work, and tools to work withall, for those who will, and blessed are the horny hands of toil.--Lowell

Beloved, let us love so well, Our work shall still be better for our love, And still our love be sweeter for our work, And both, commended, for the sake of each, By all true workers and true lovers born. --Elizabeth B. Browning